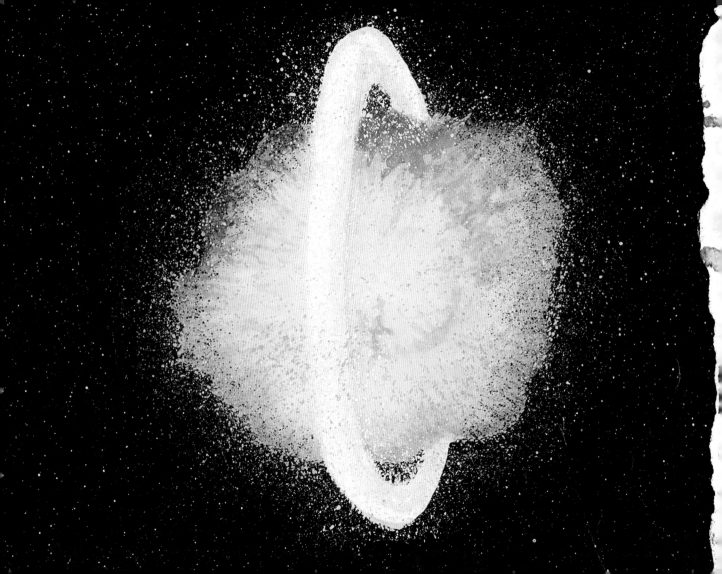

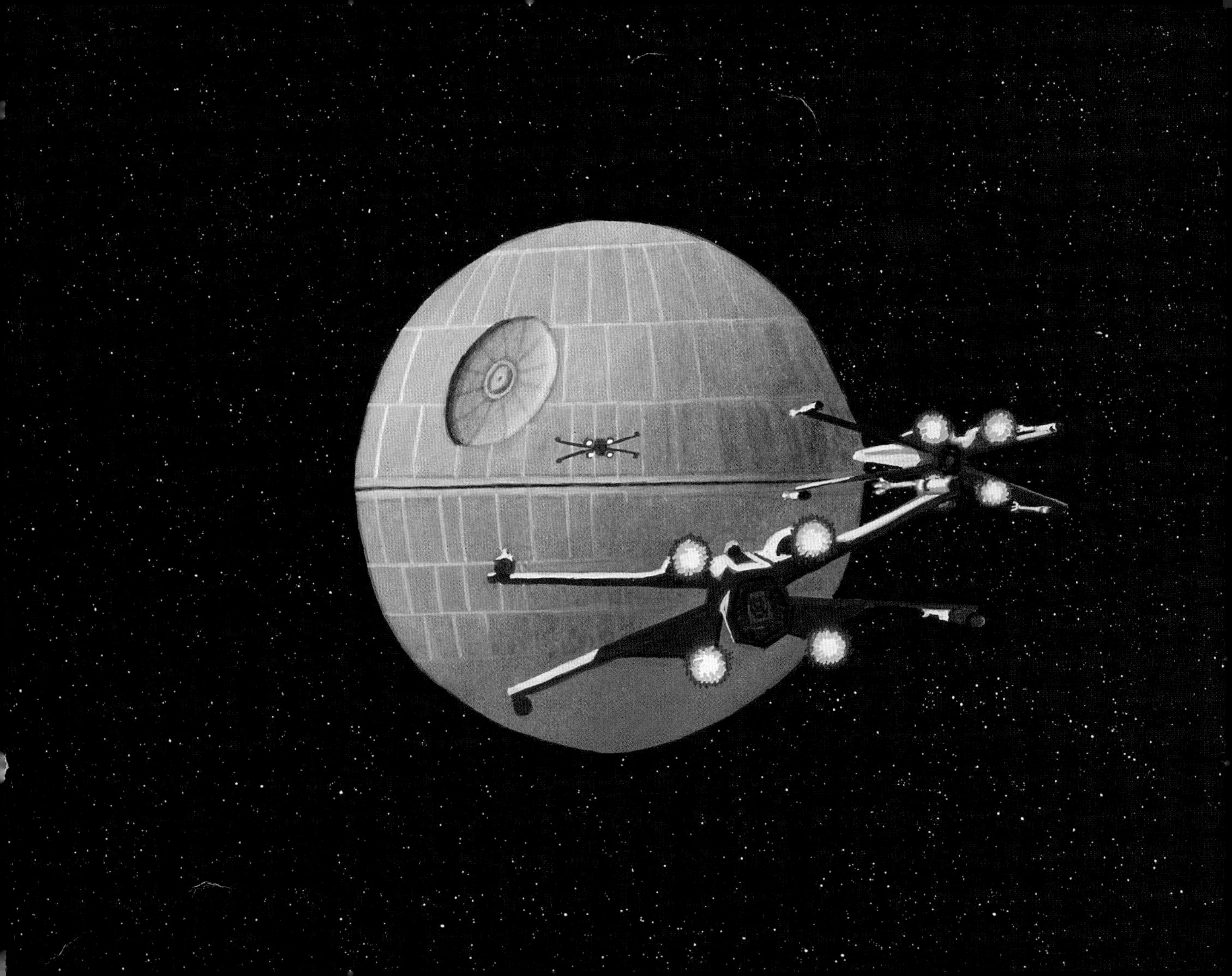

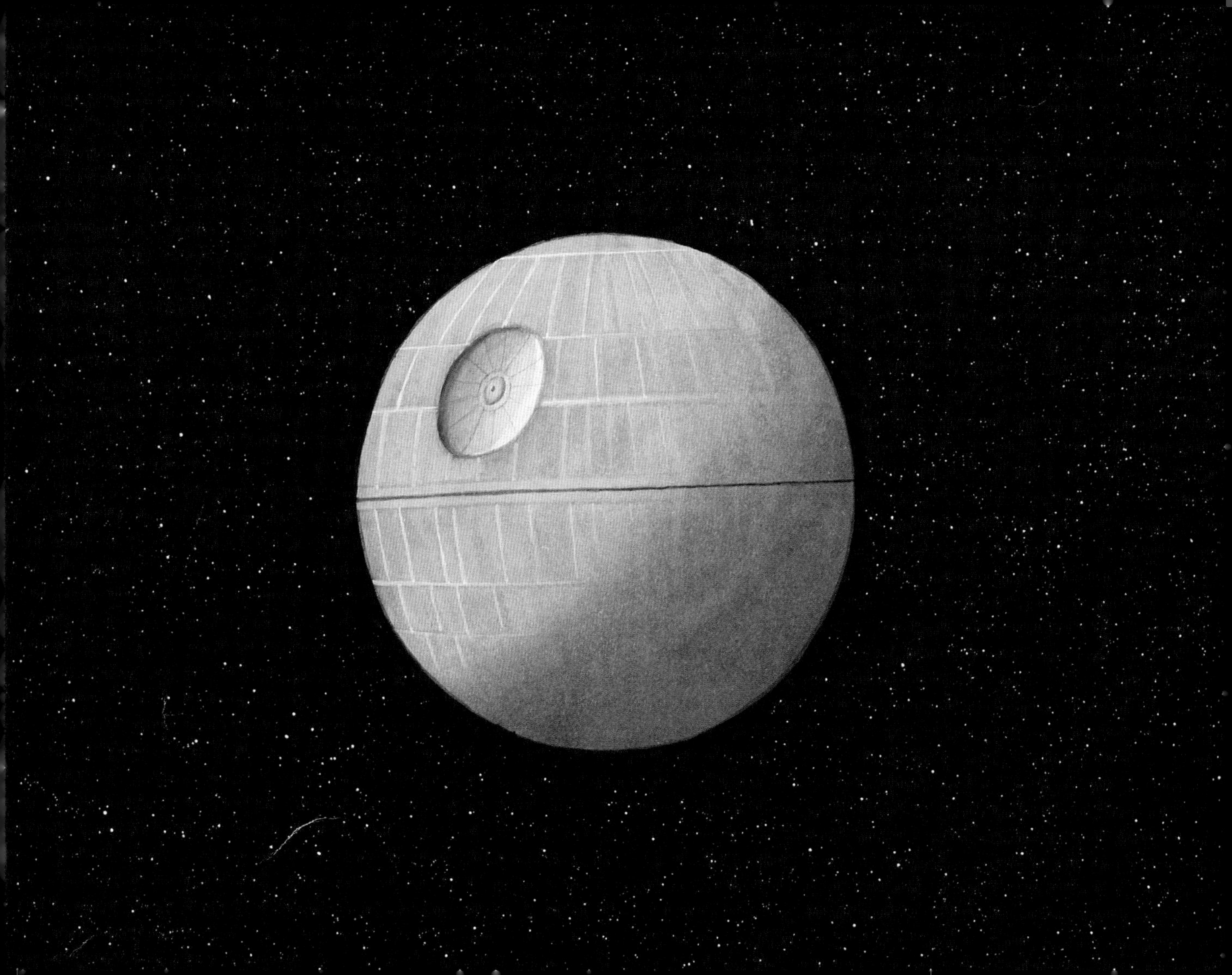

On the Death Star.

And the last stormtrooper lives happily ever after.

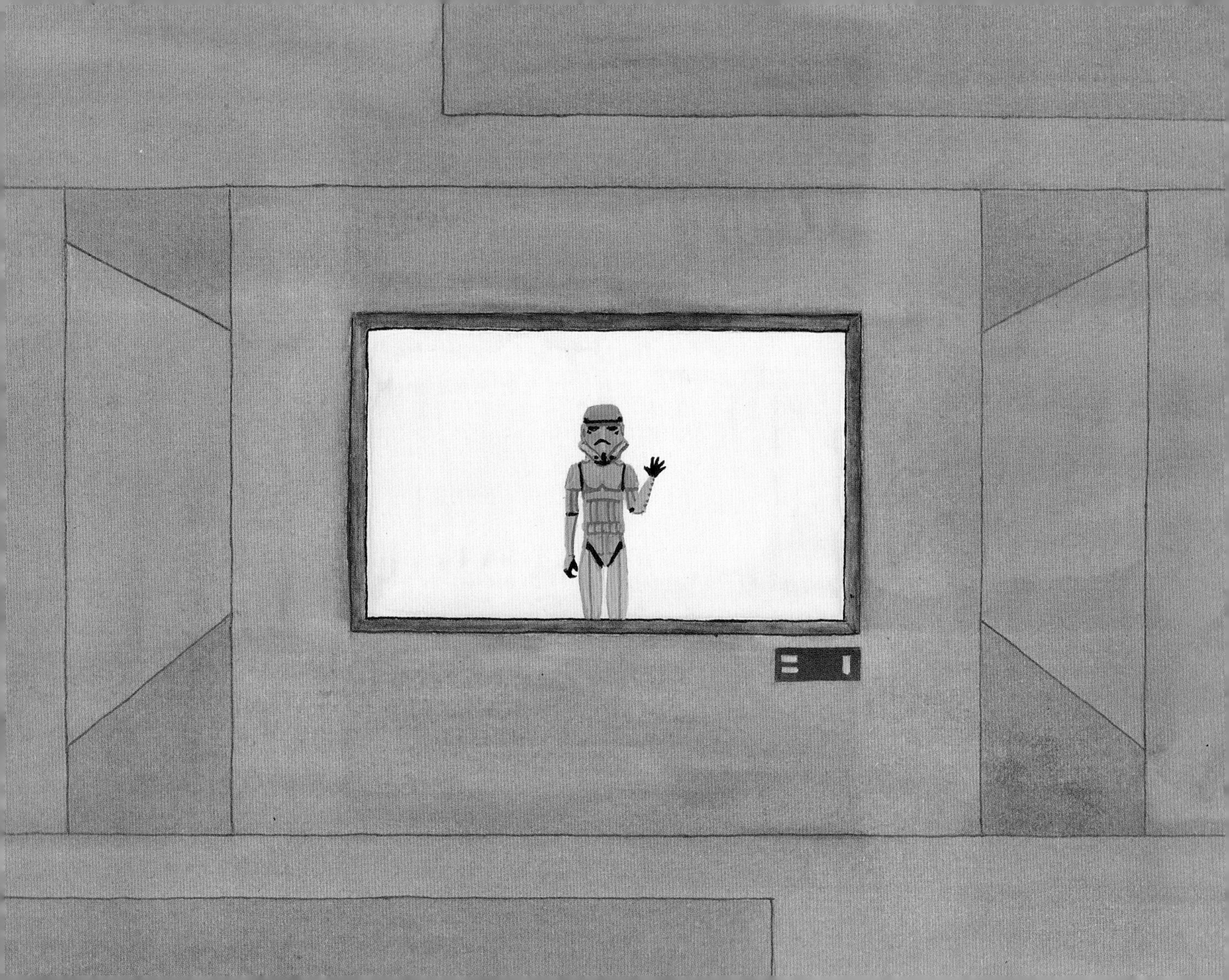

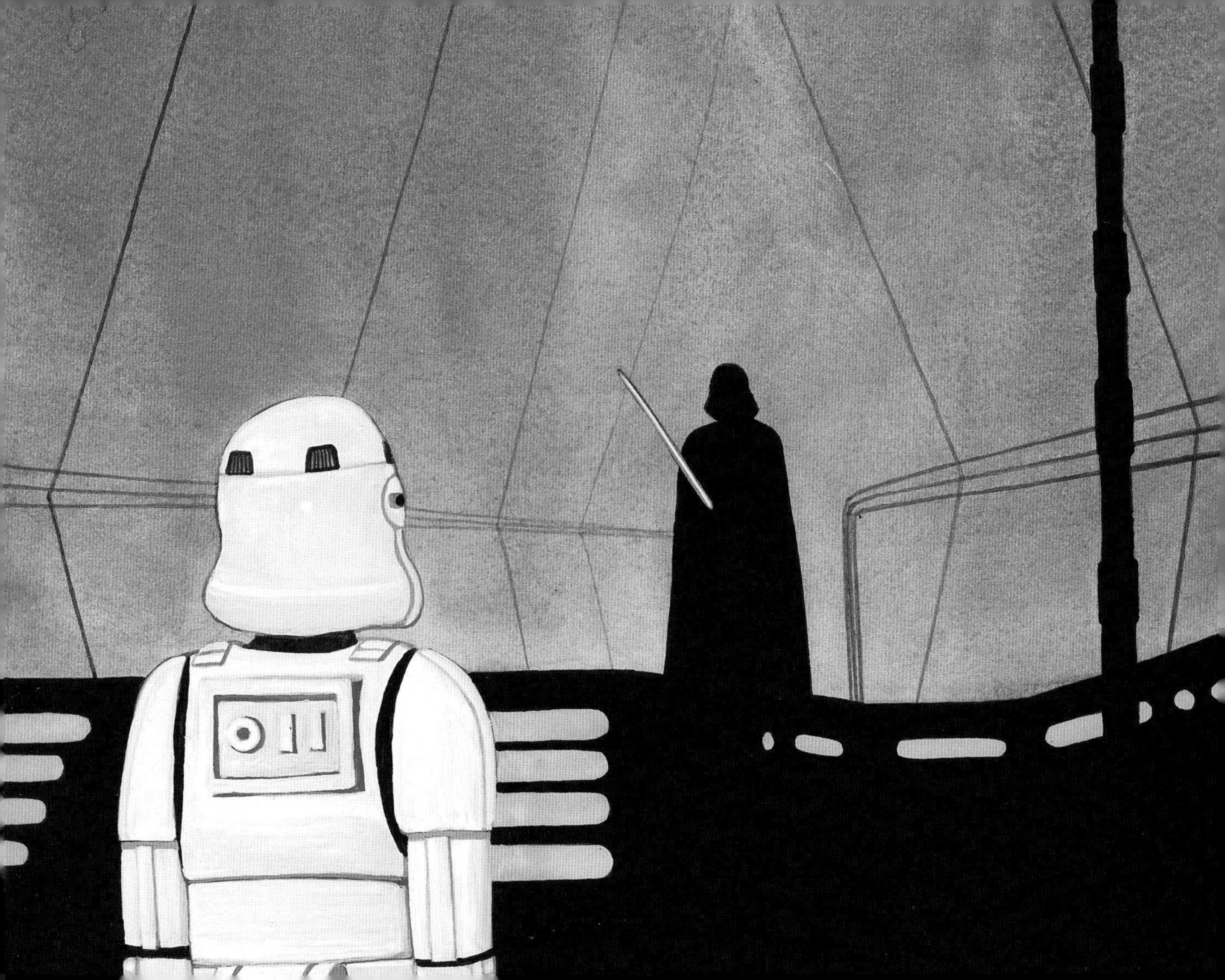

One stormtrooper fails Lord Vader for the last time.

Two stormtroopers get Jedi mind-tricked.

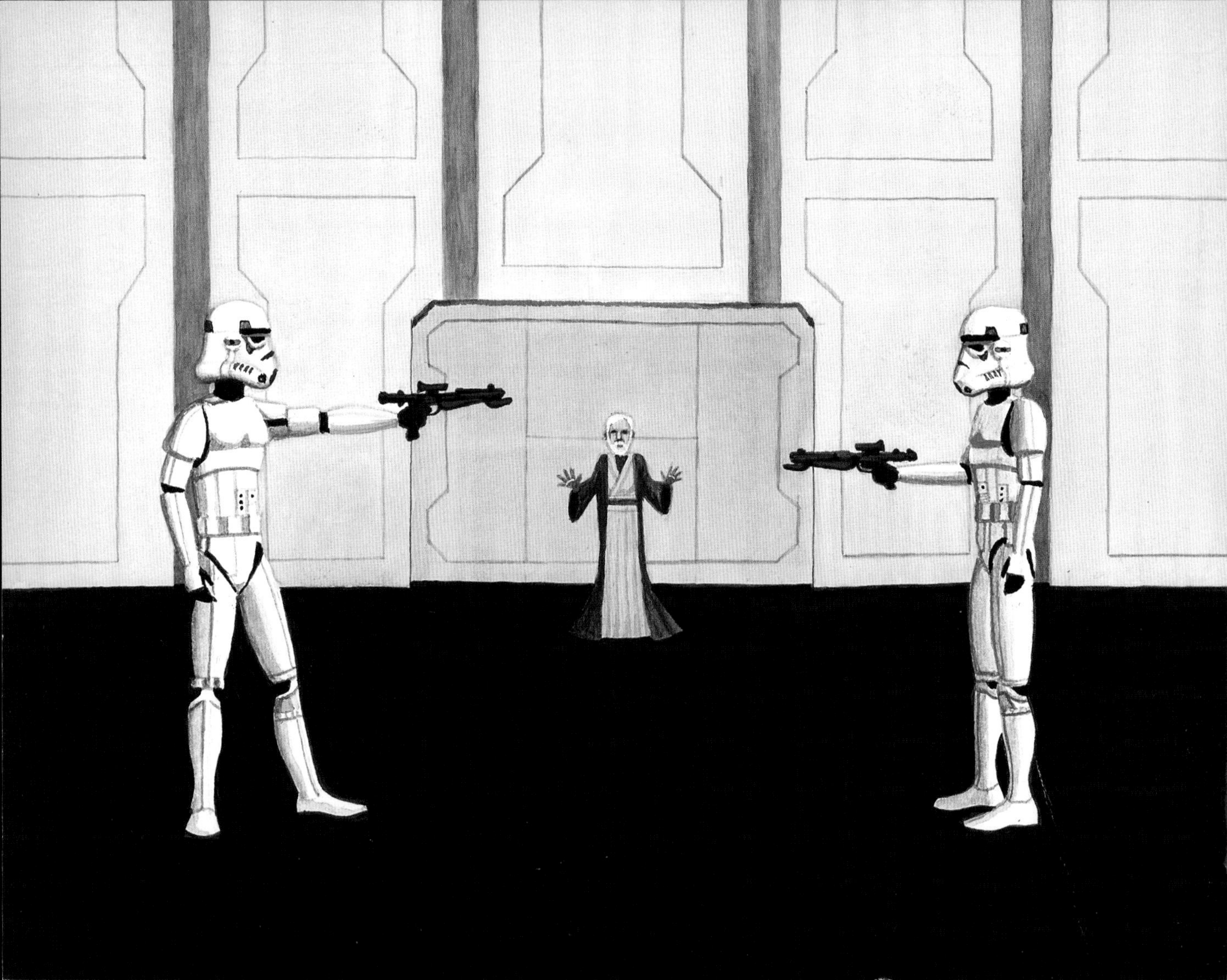

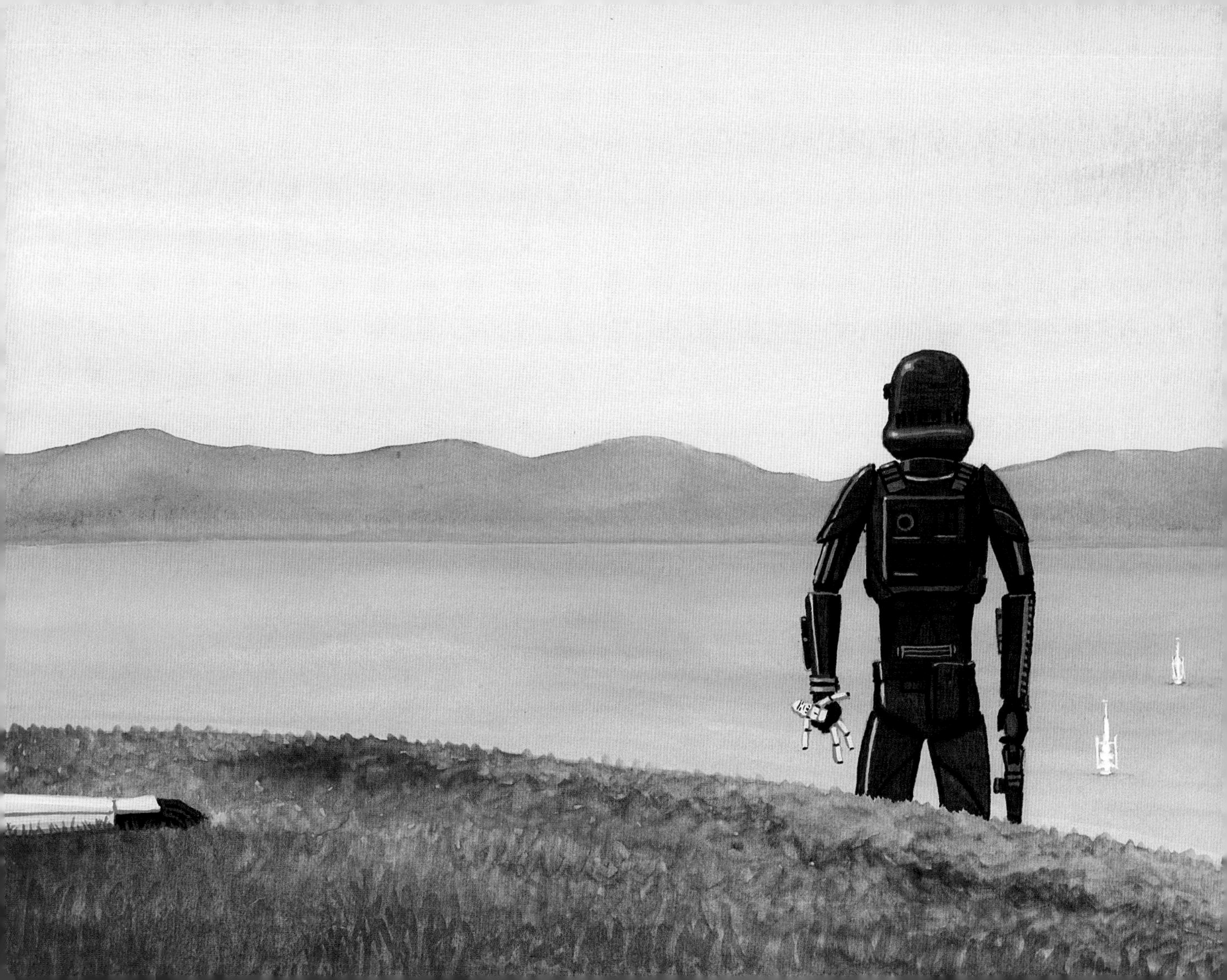

One stormtrooper teases a death trooper for playing with dolls.

Three stormtroopers become scout troopers.

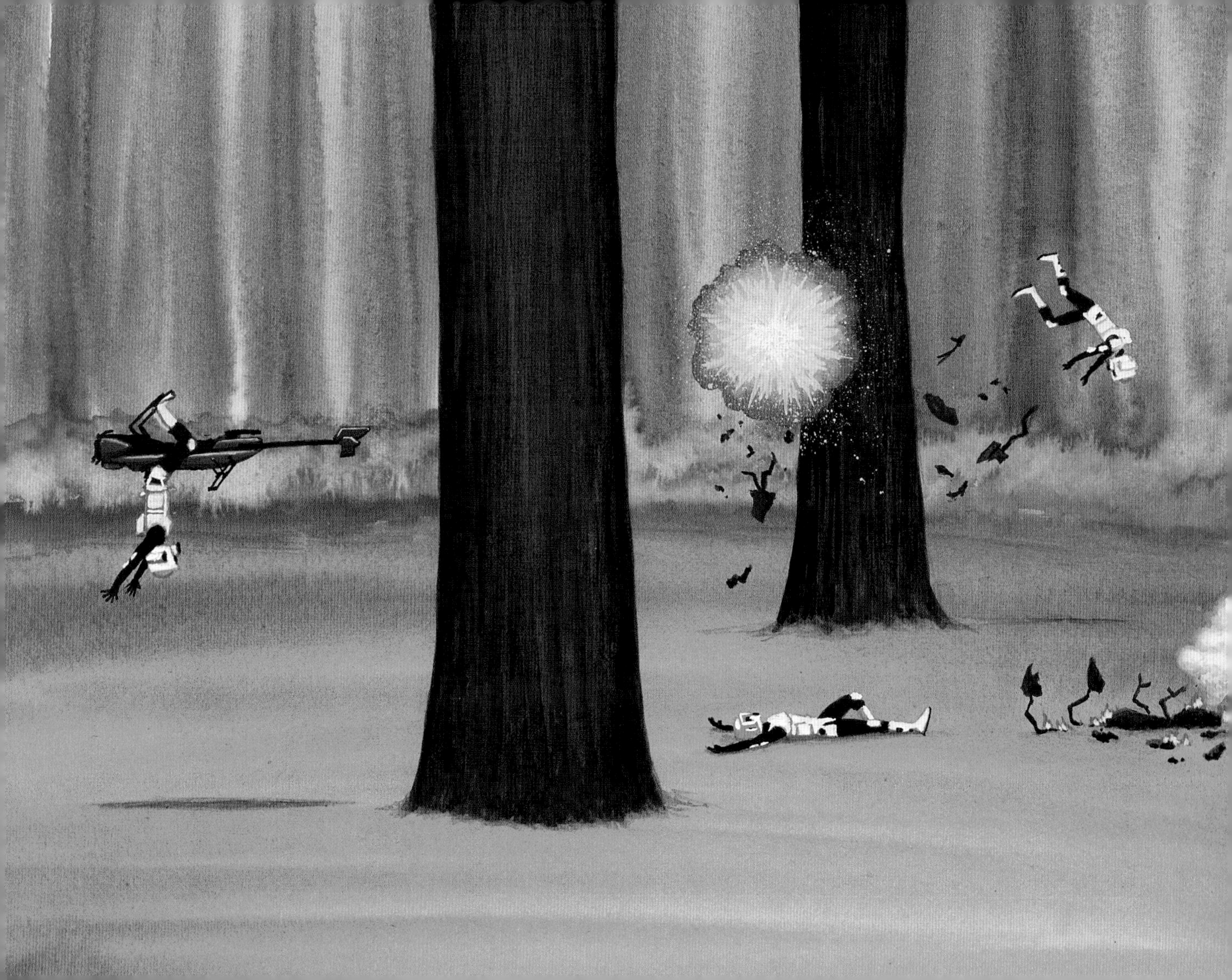

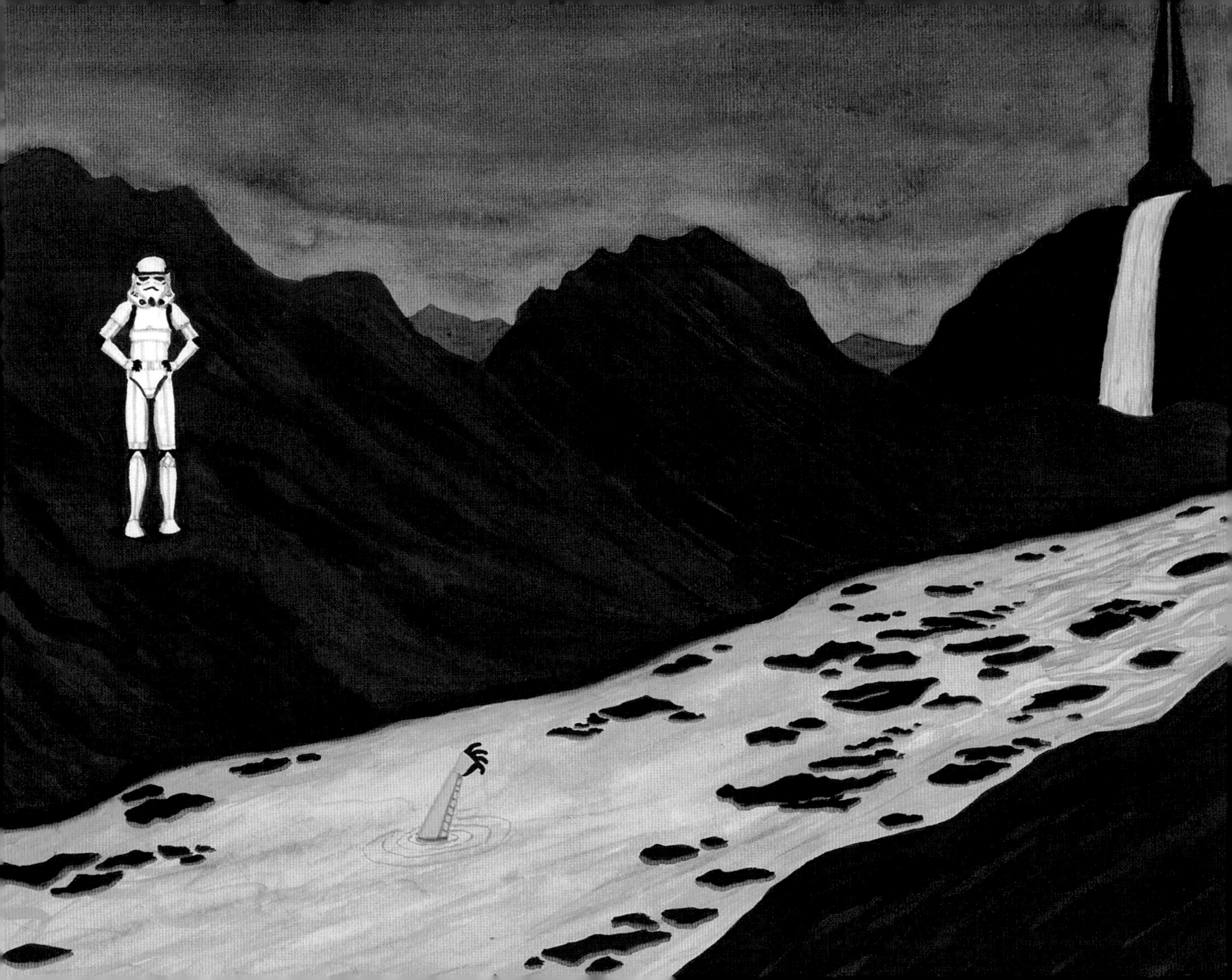

One stormtrooper fails to get to higher ground.

One stormtrooper realizes too late that it's a trap.

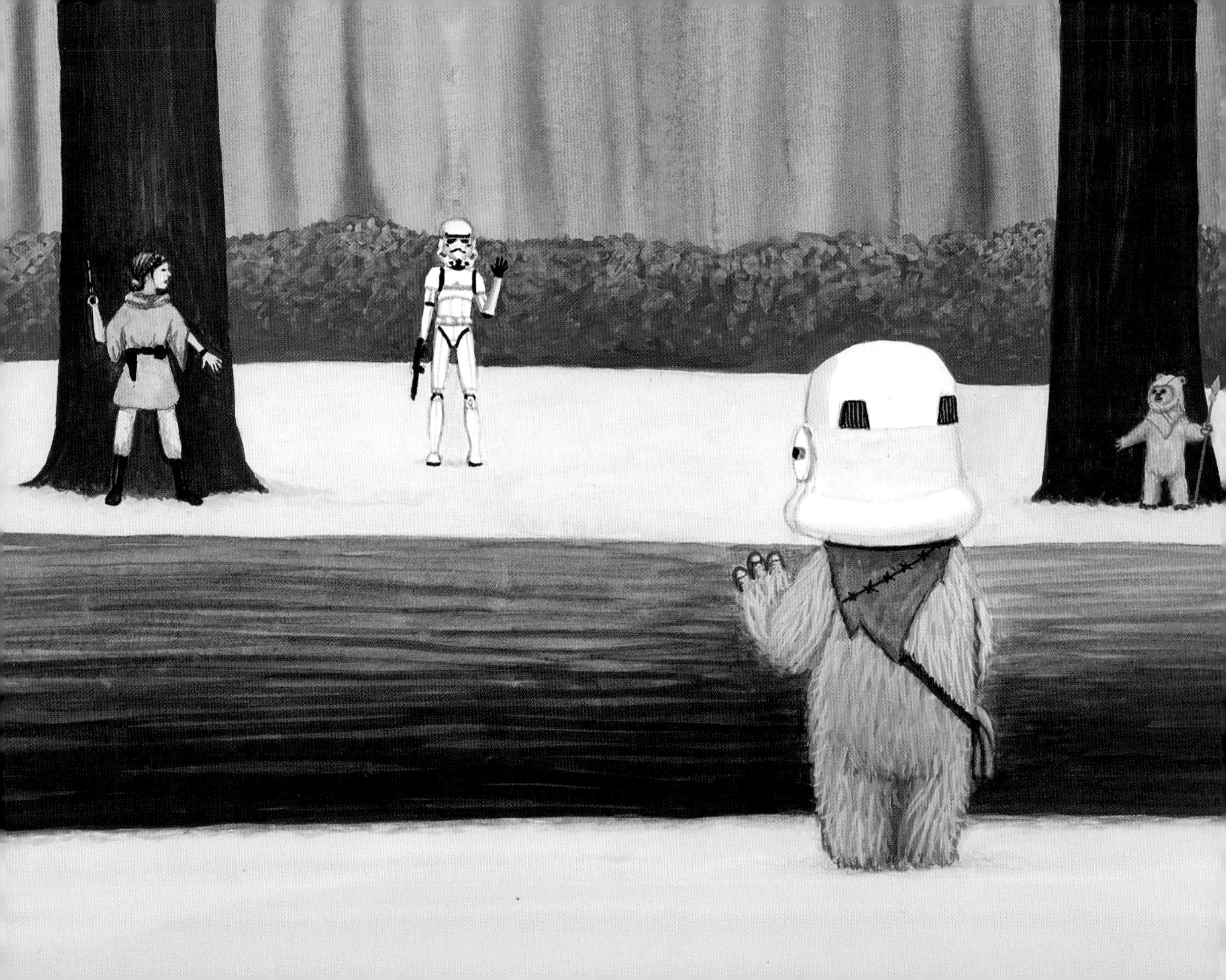

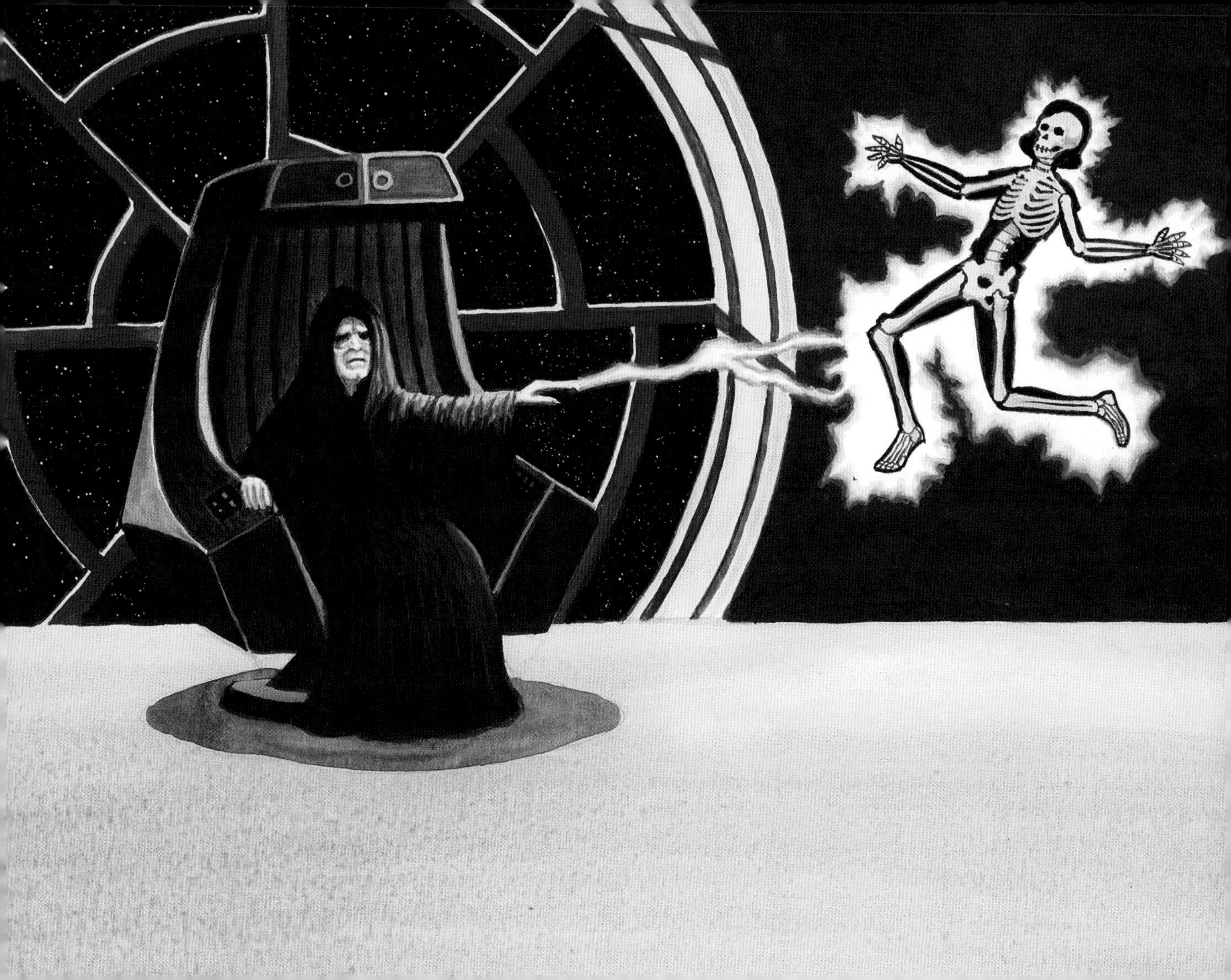

One stormtrooper informs the Emperor that the Death Star plans have been stolen. Again.

Two stormtroopers lose their armor and are sent to the spice mines of Kessel.

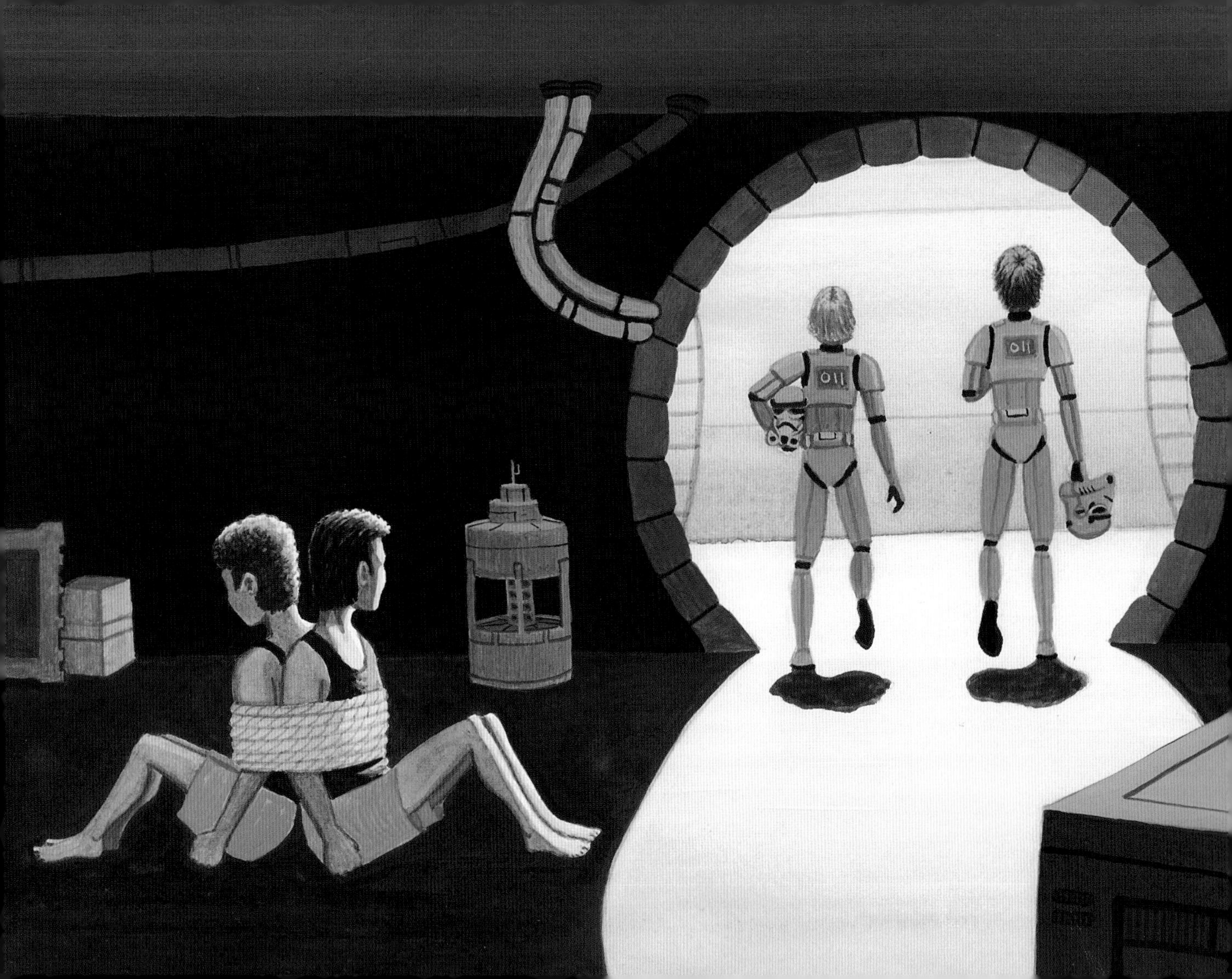
011
011

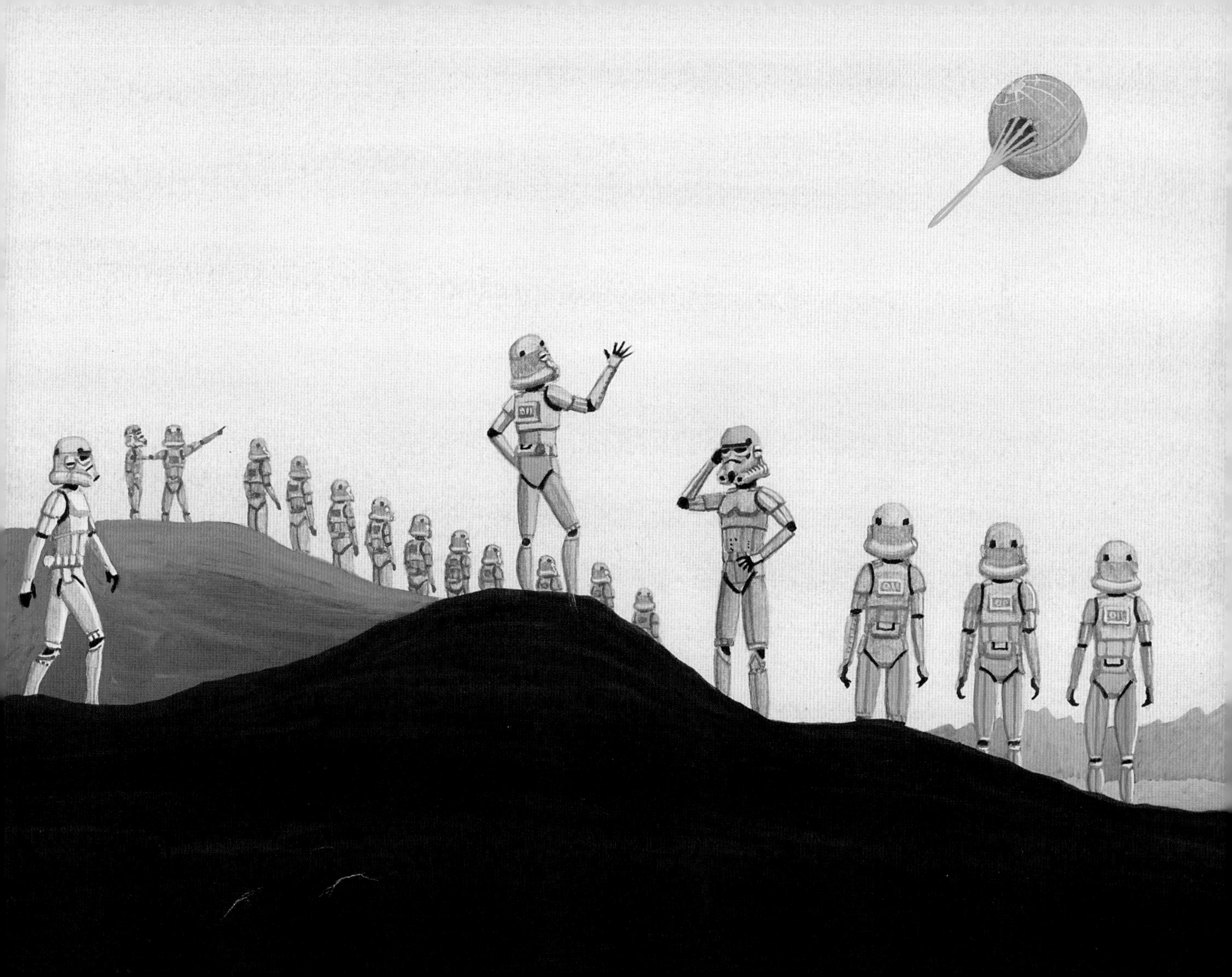

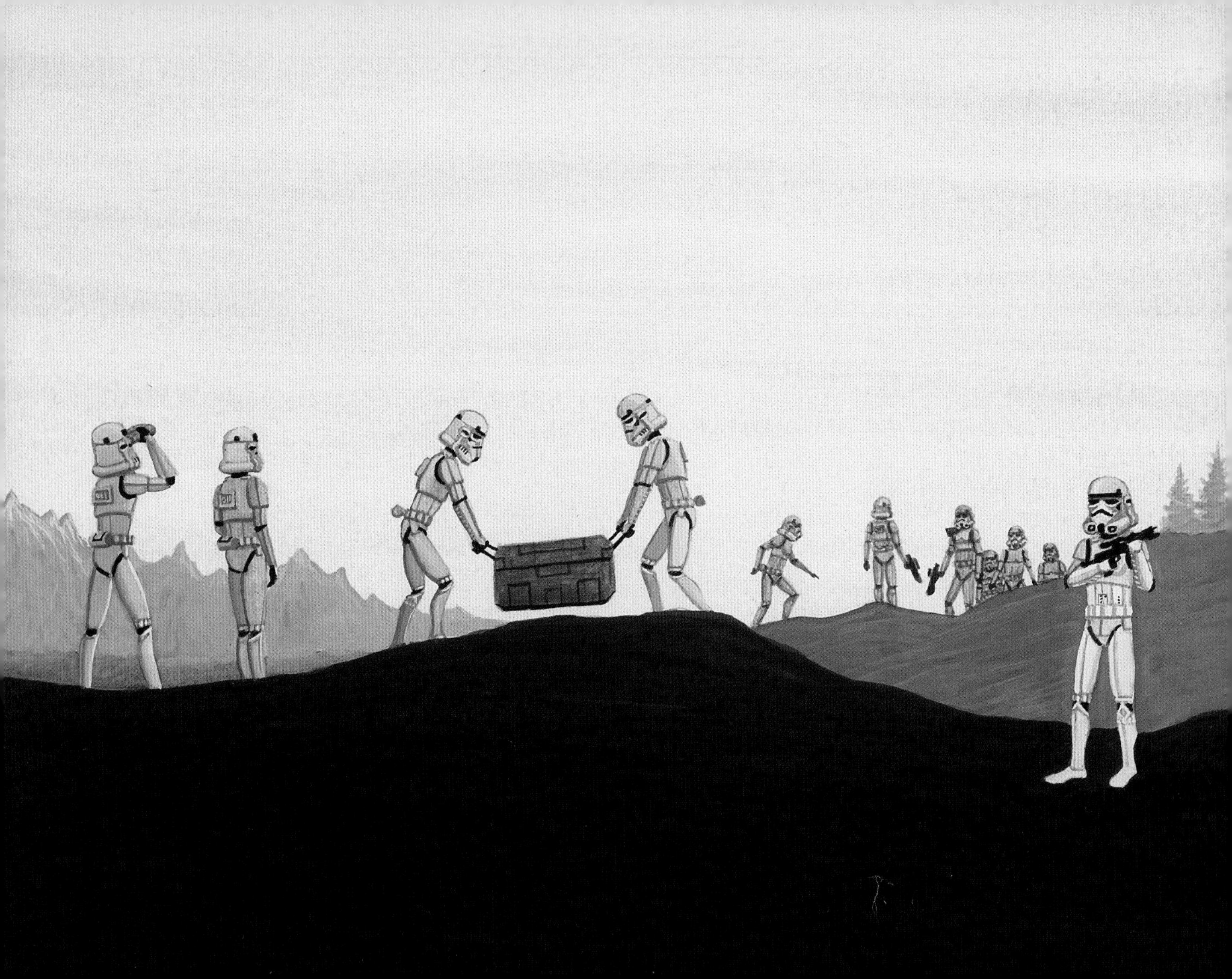

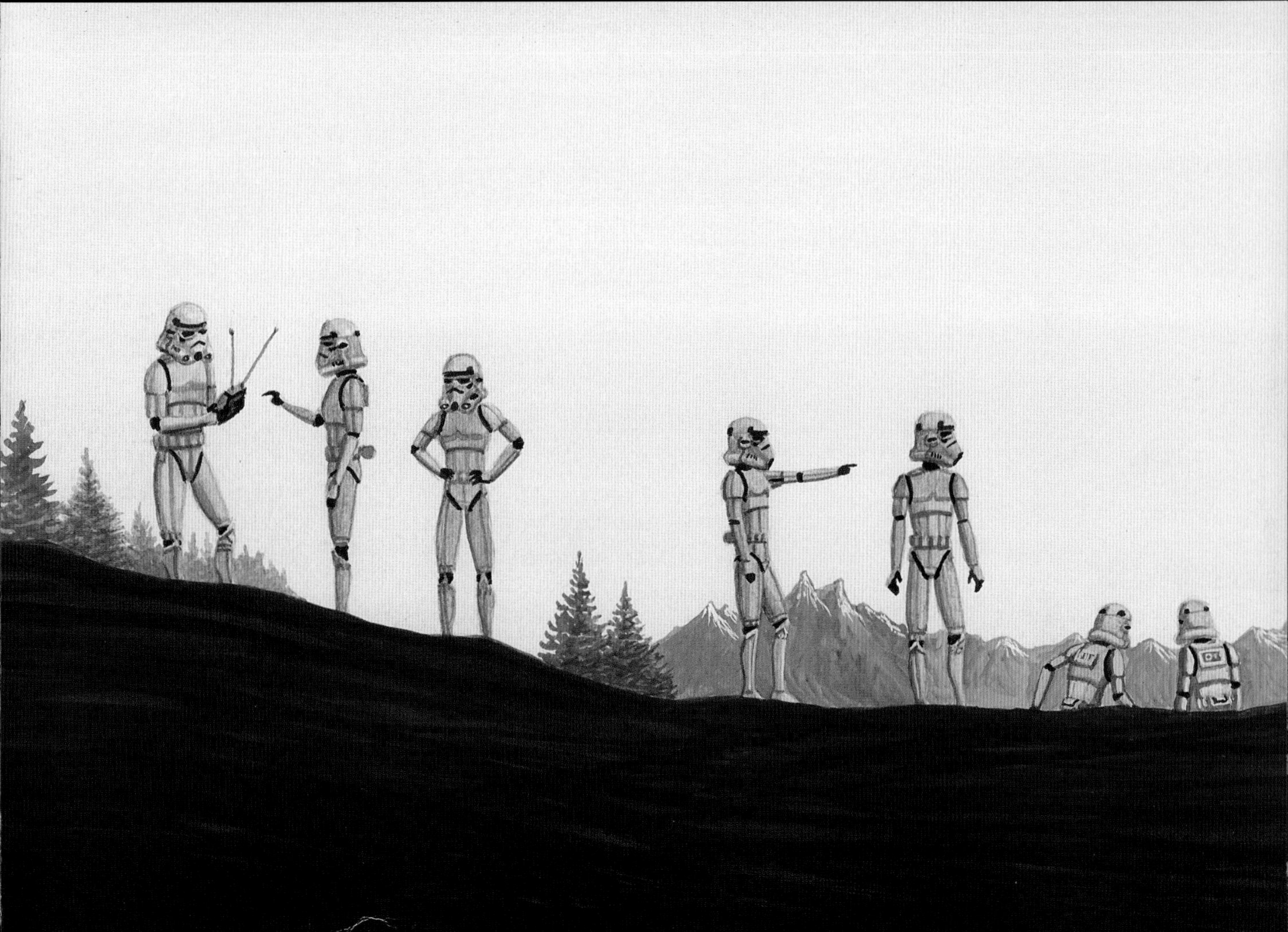

Thirty-six stormtroopers are stationed on Alderaan.

One stormtrooper juggles thermal detonators to impress a girl.

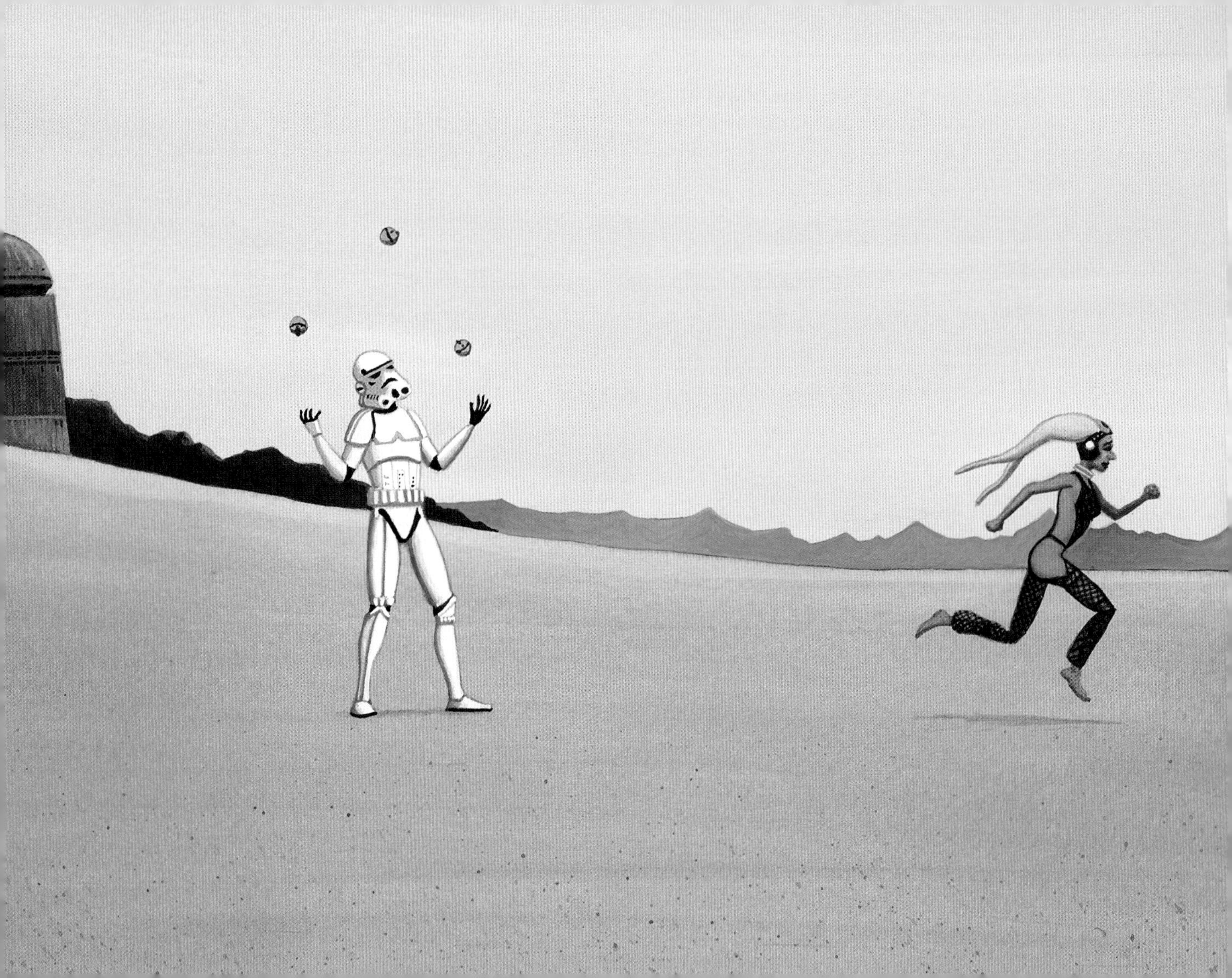

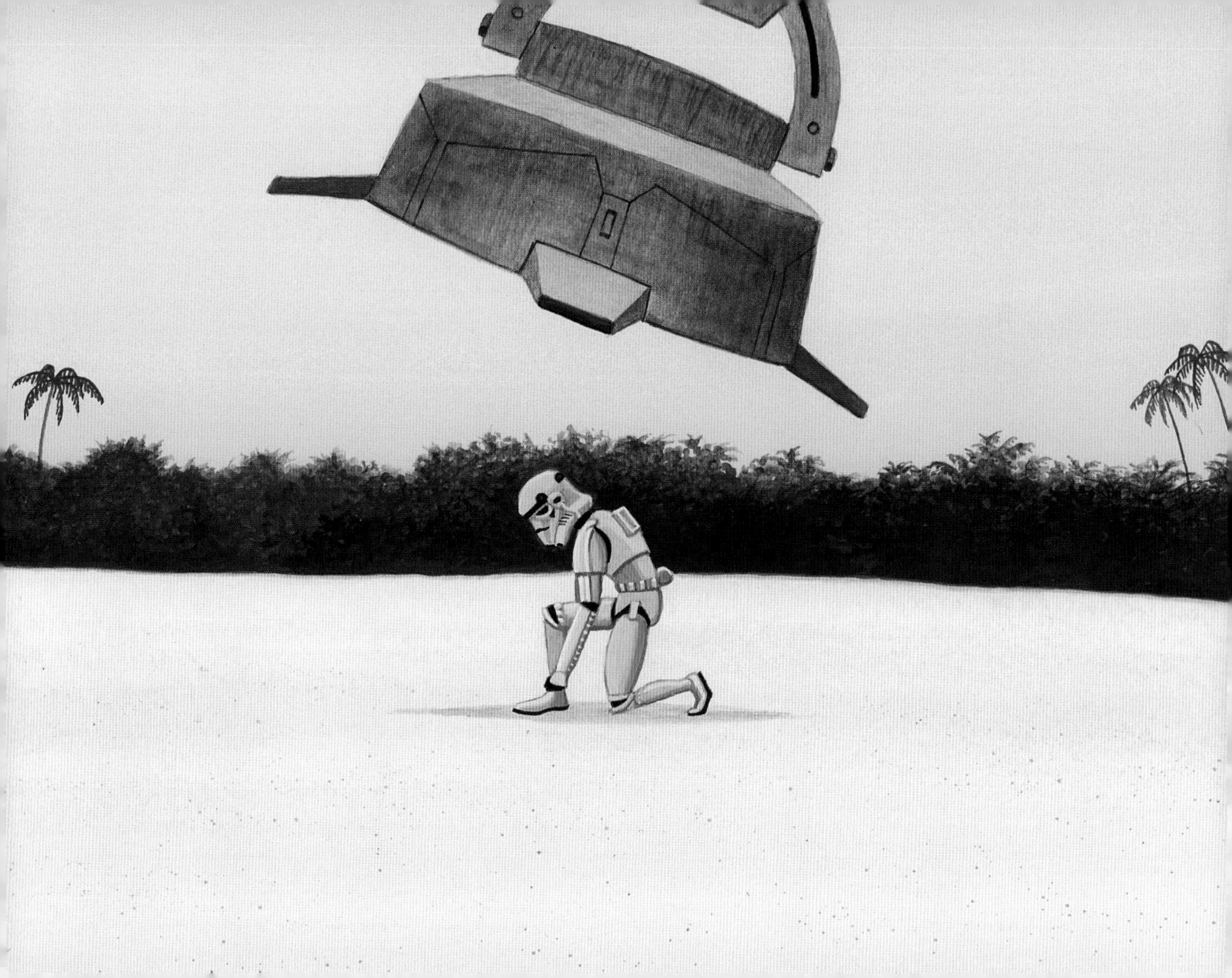

One stormtrooper gets a pebble in his boot.

One stormtrooper forgets his grappling hook.

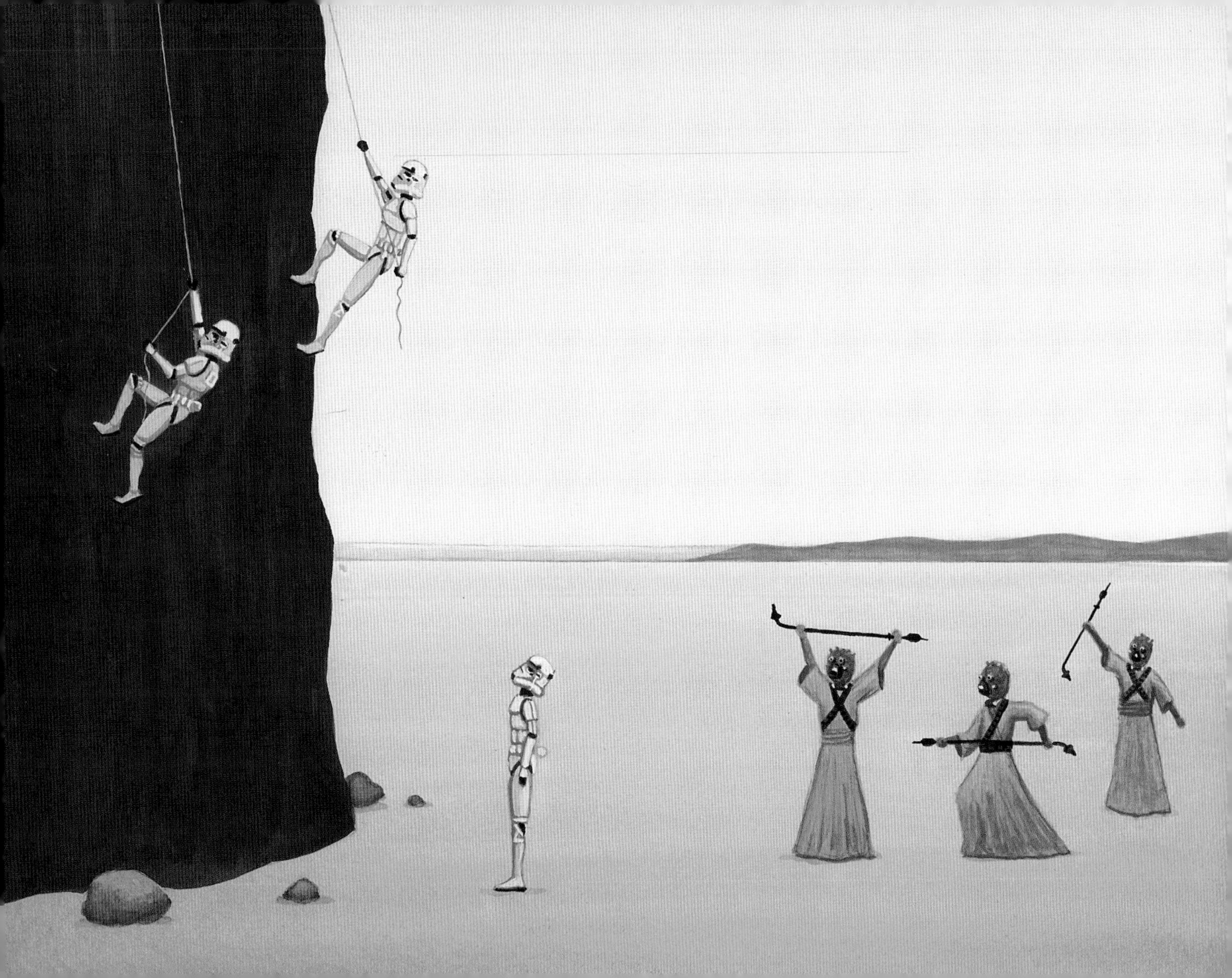

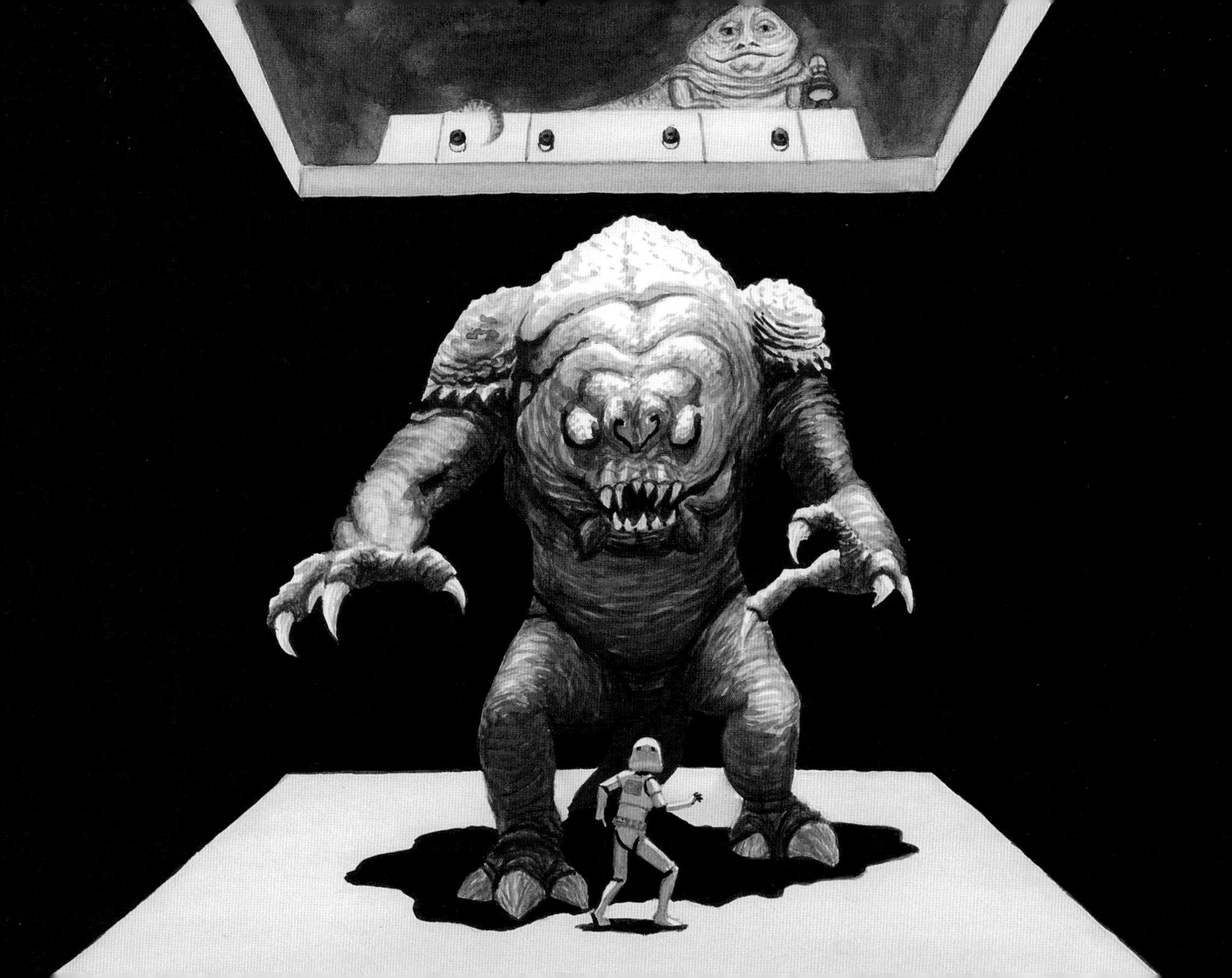

One stormtrooper fails to show Jabba the proper respect.

Three stormtroopers think they can make the jump.

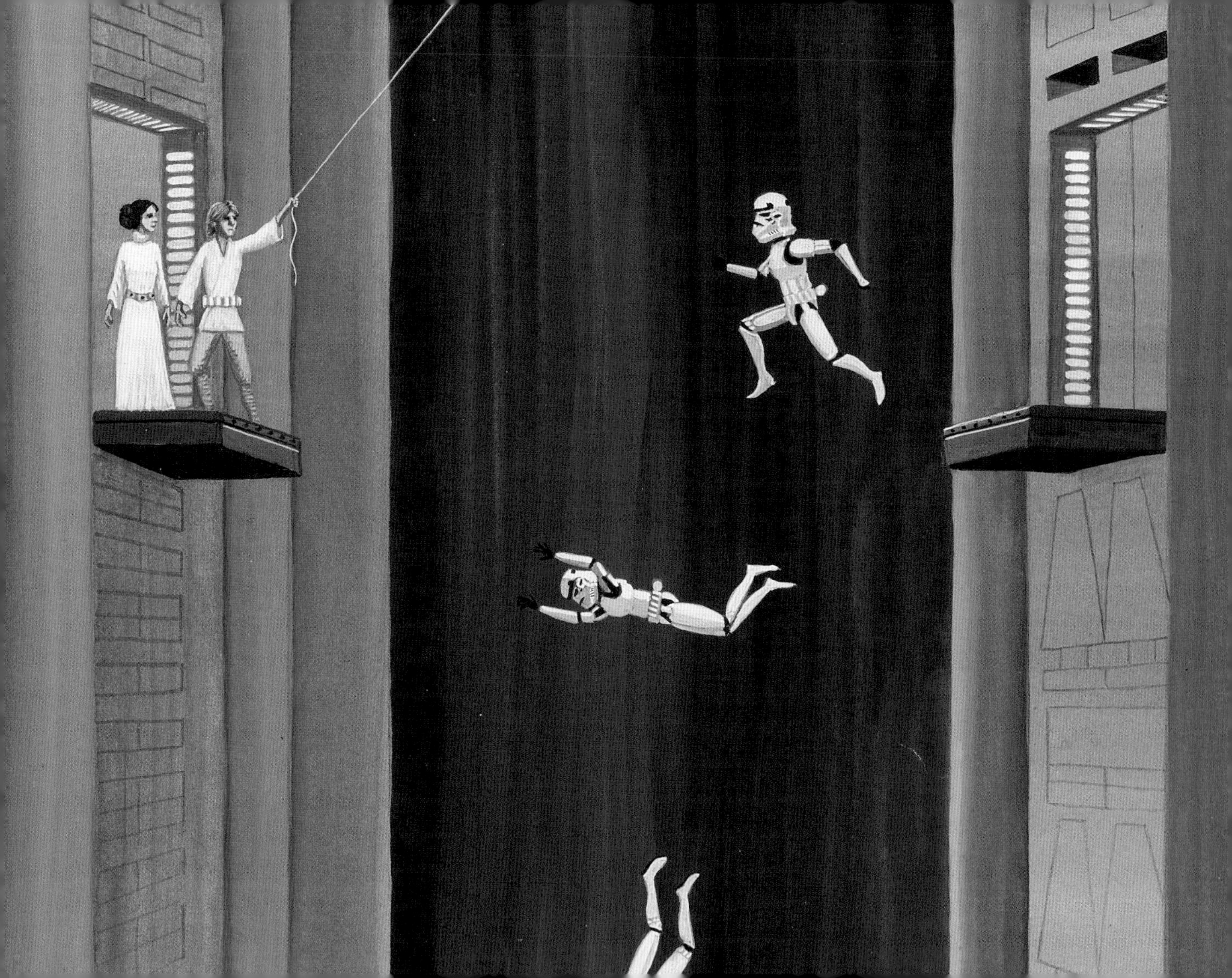

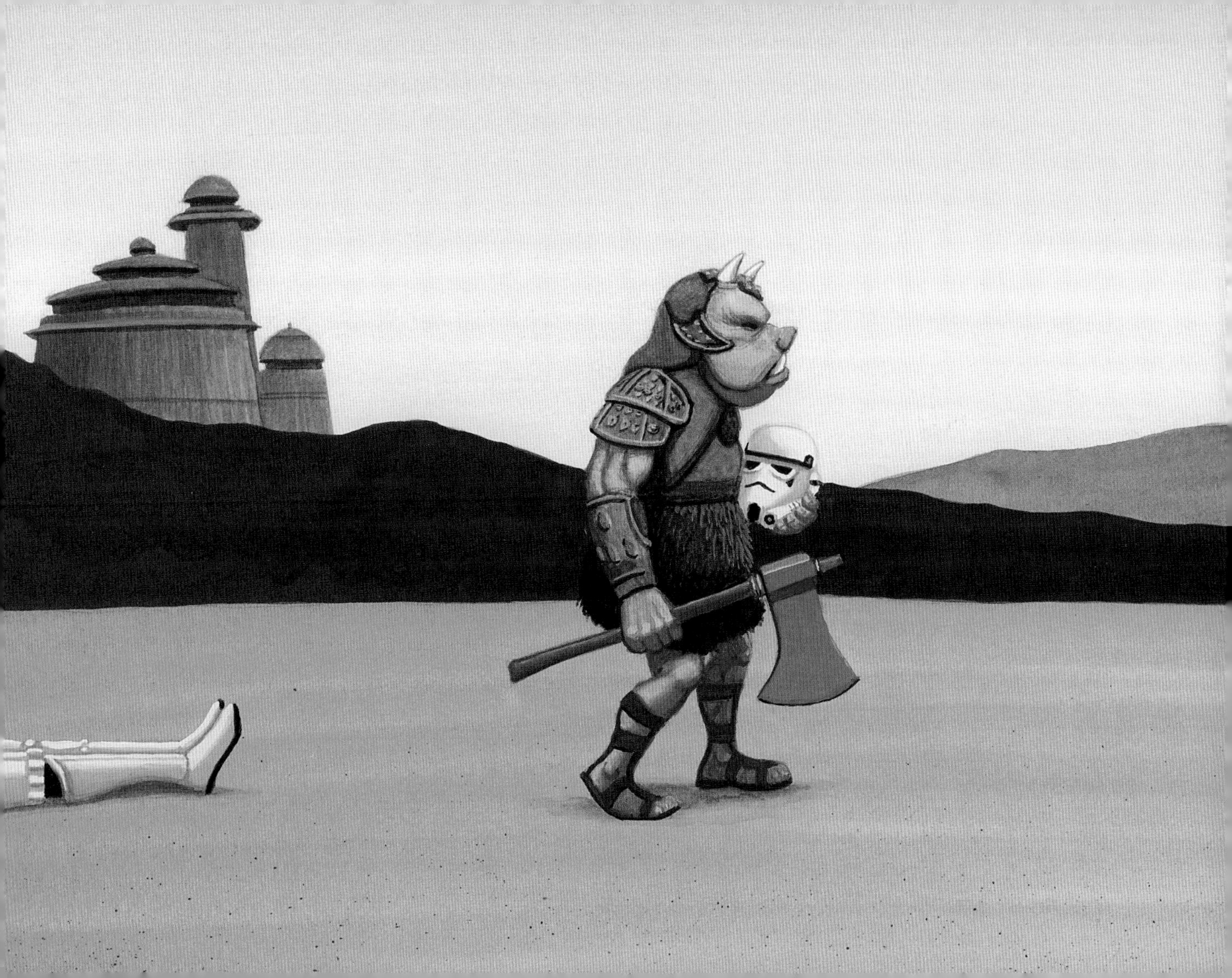

One stormtrooper makes fun of a Gamorrean.

One stormtrooper gets caught after a joy ride.

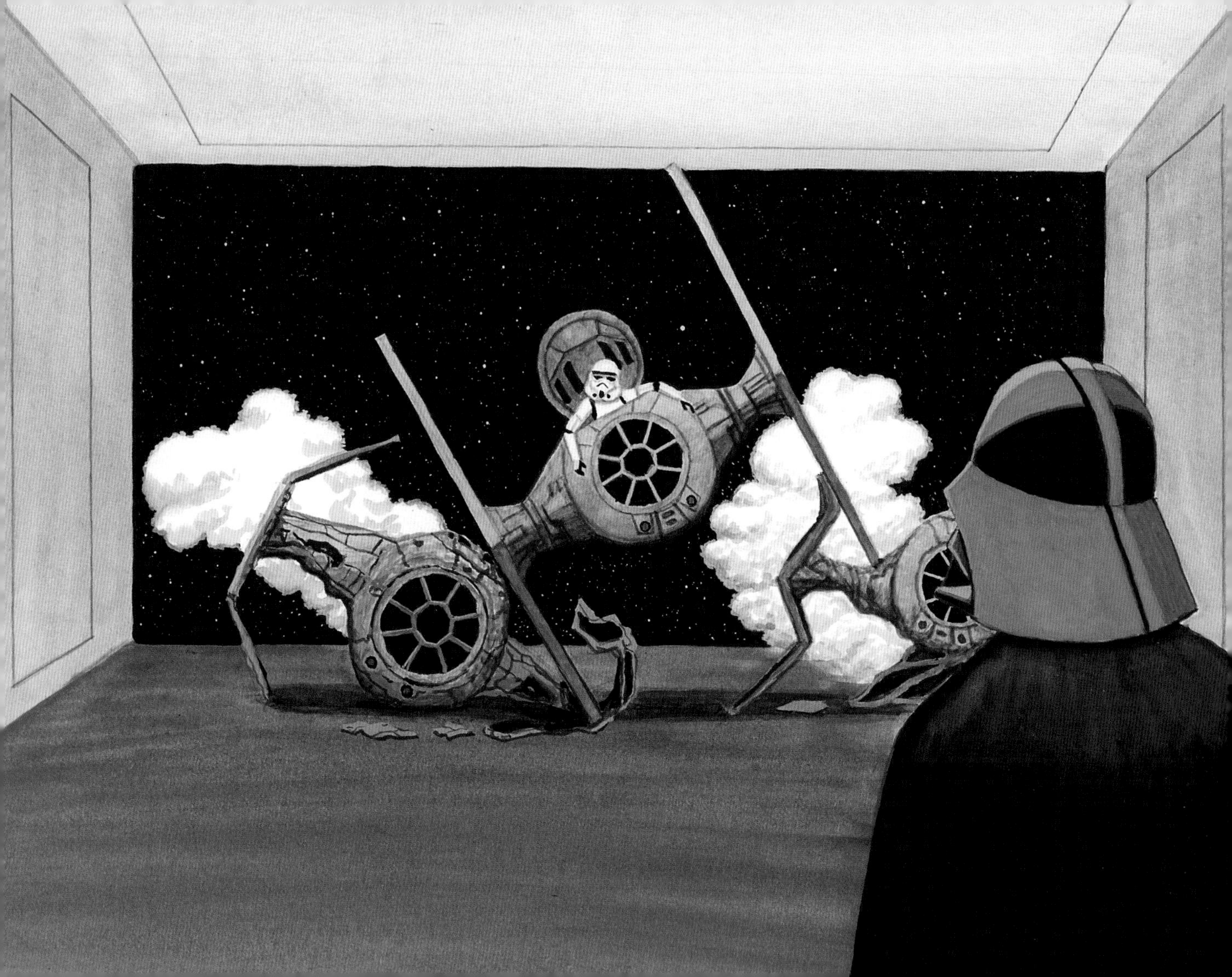

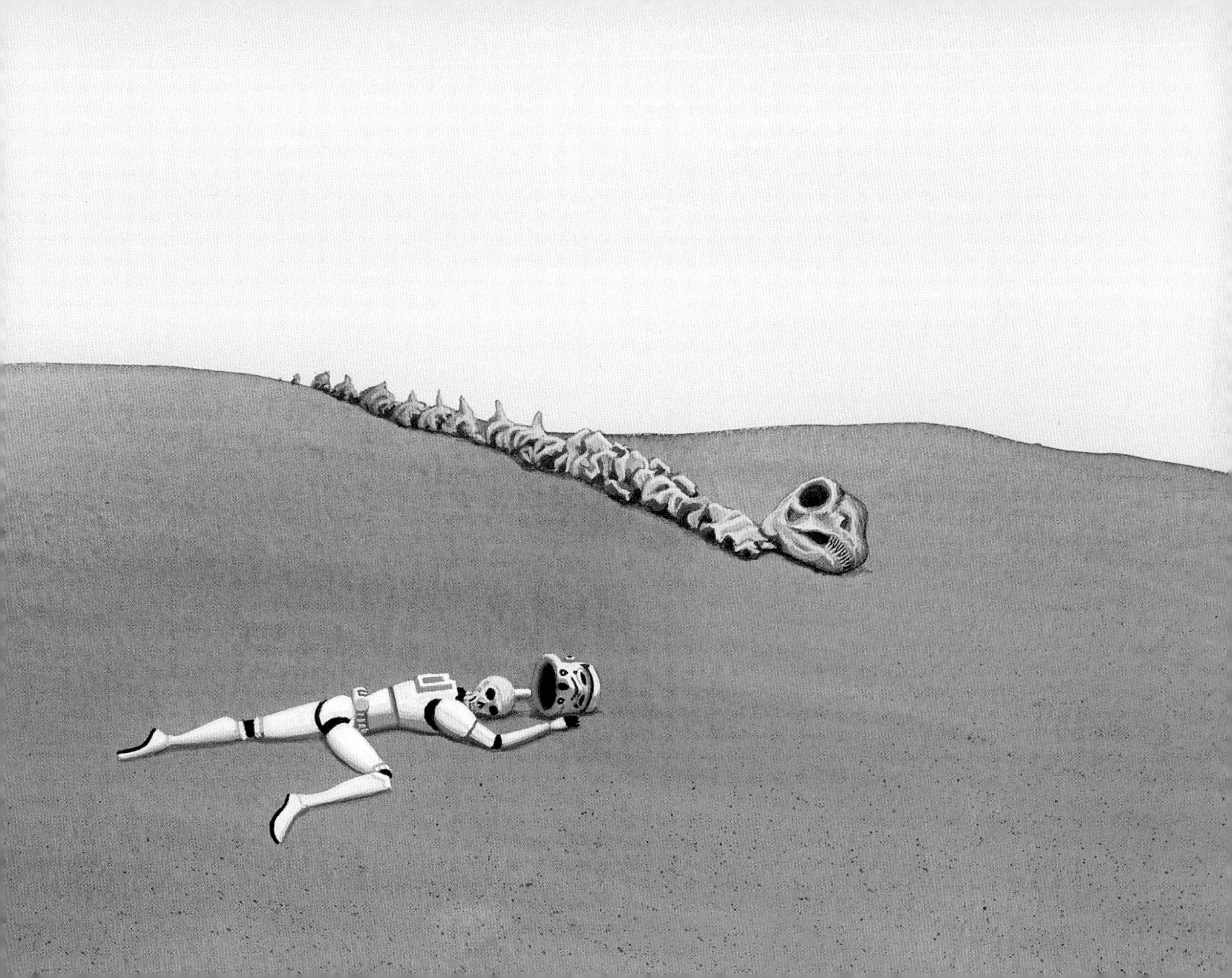

One stormtrooper never finds the droids he was looking for.

One stormtrooper displeases Lord Vader two systems away.

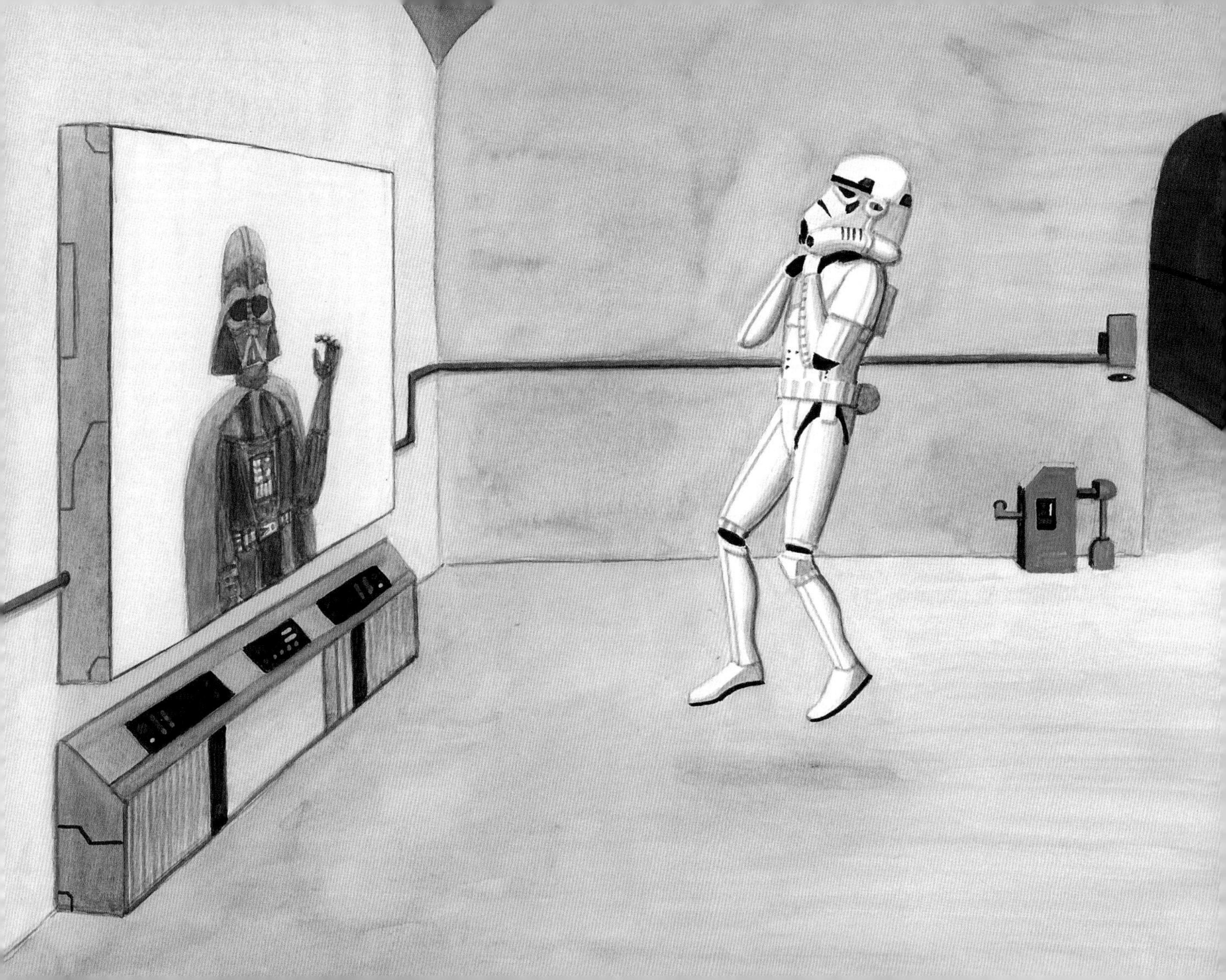

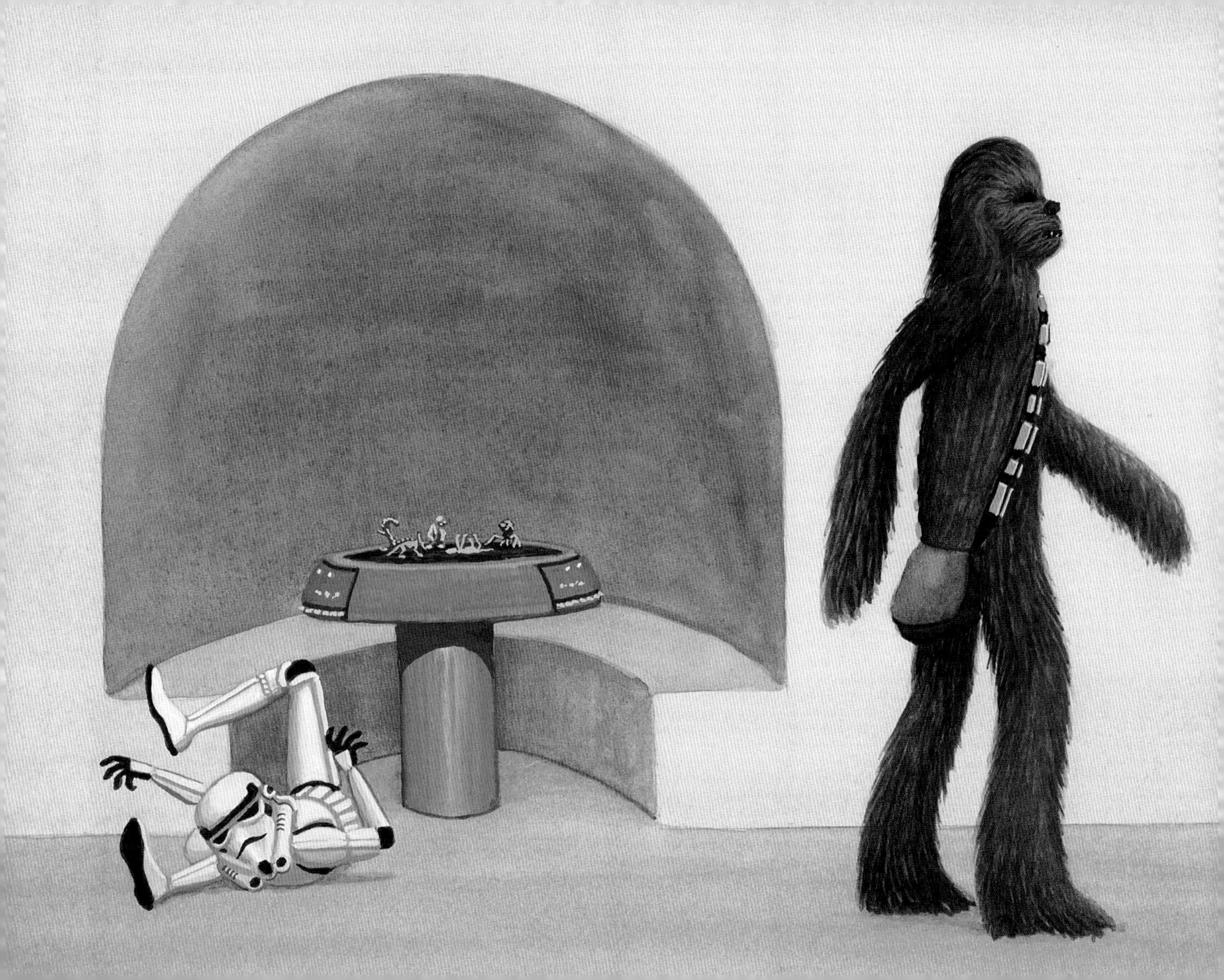

One stormtrooper doesn't let the Wookiee win.

One stormtrooper never learns to swim.

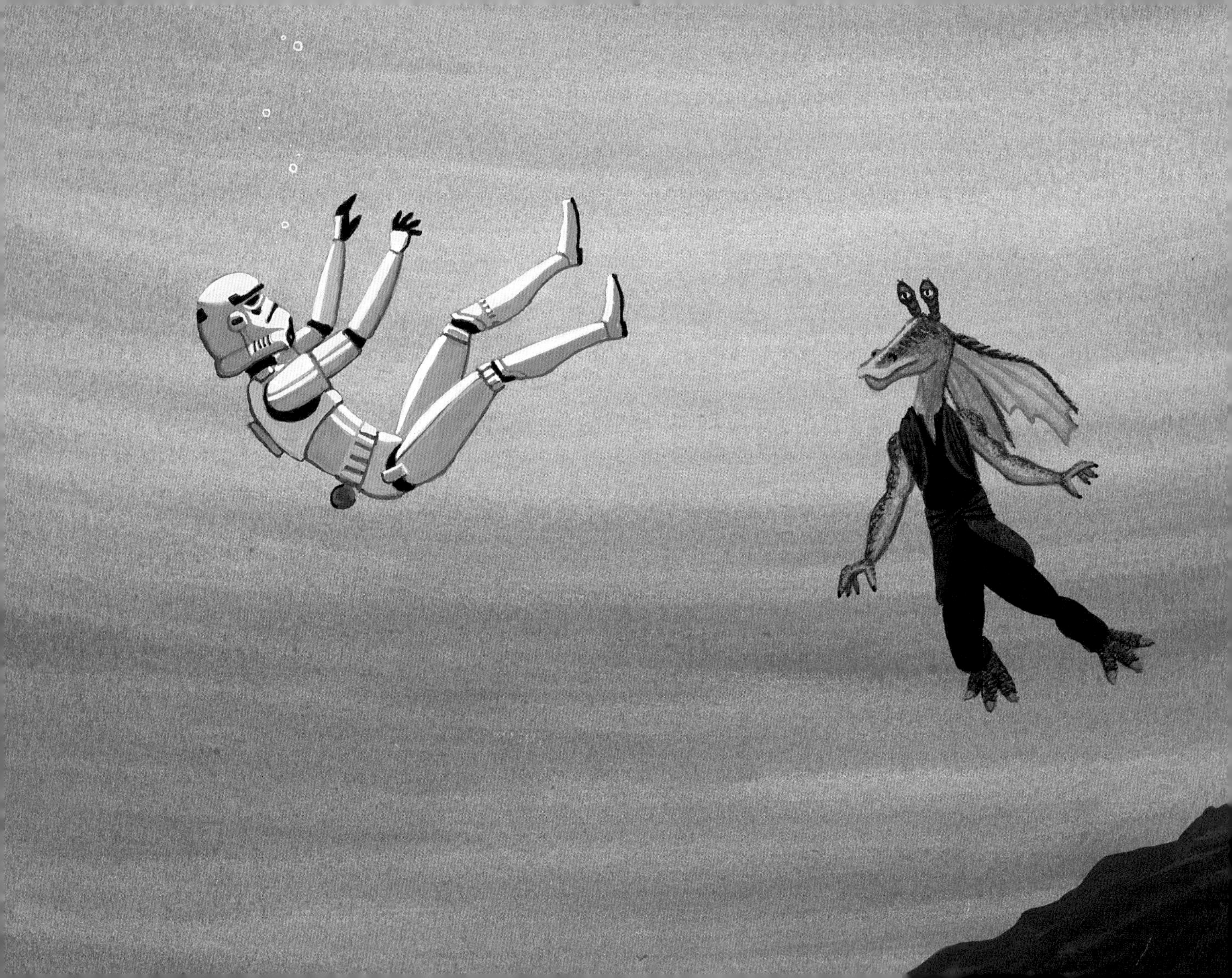

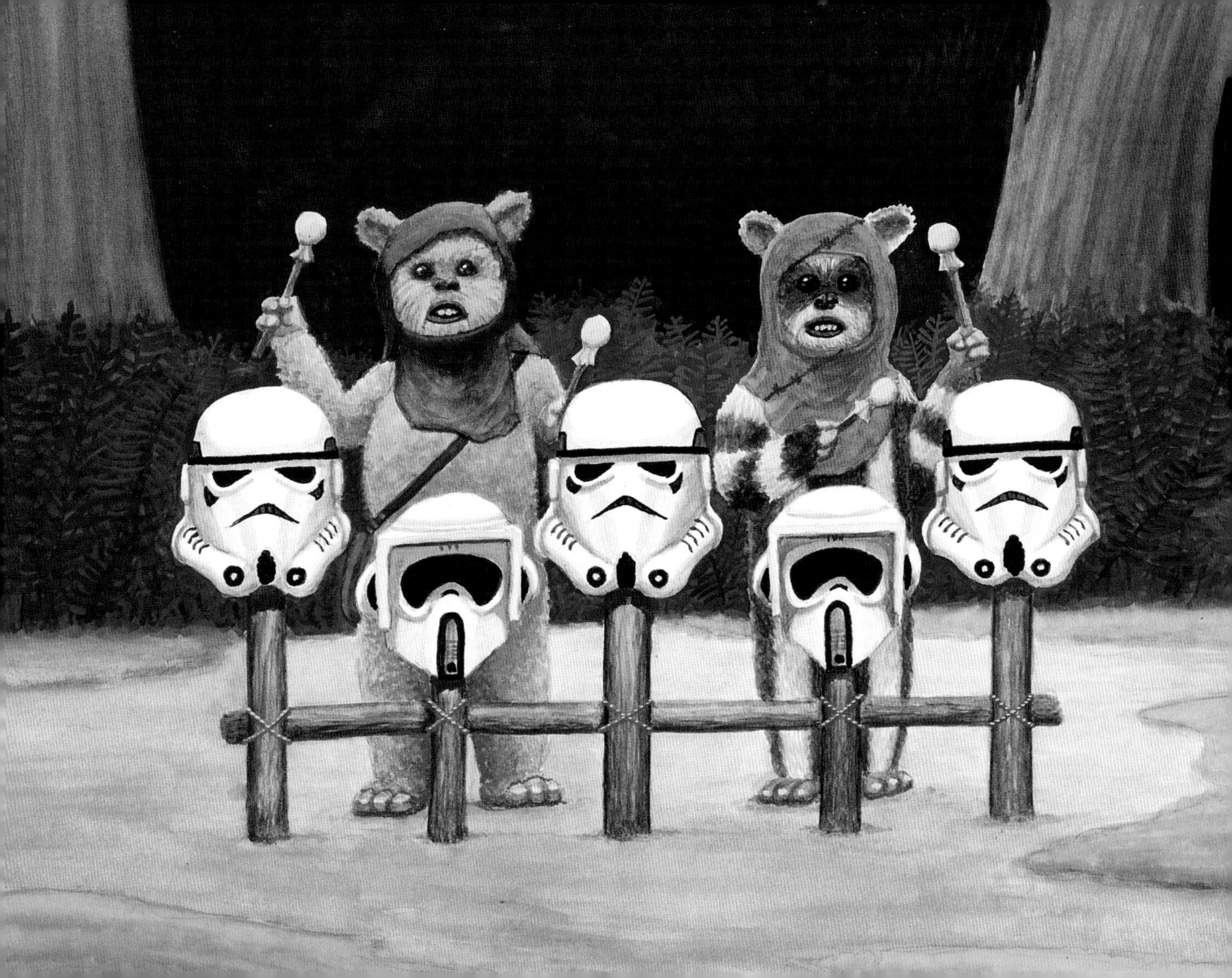

Five stormtroopers join a band.

One stormtrooper finds a jetpack.

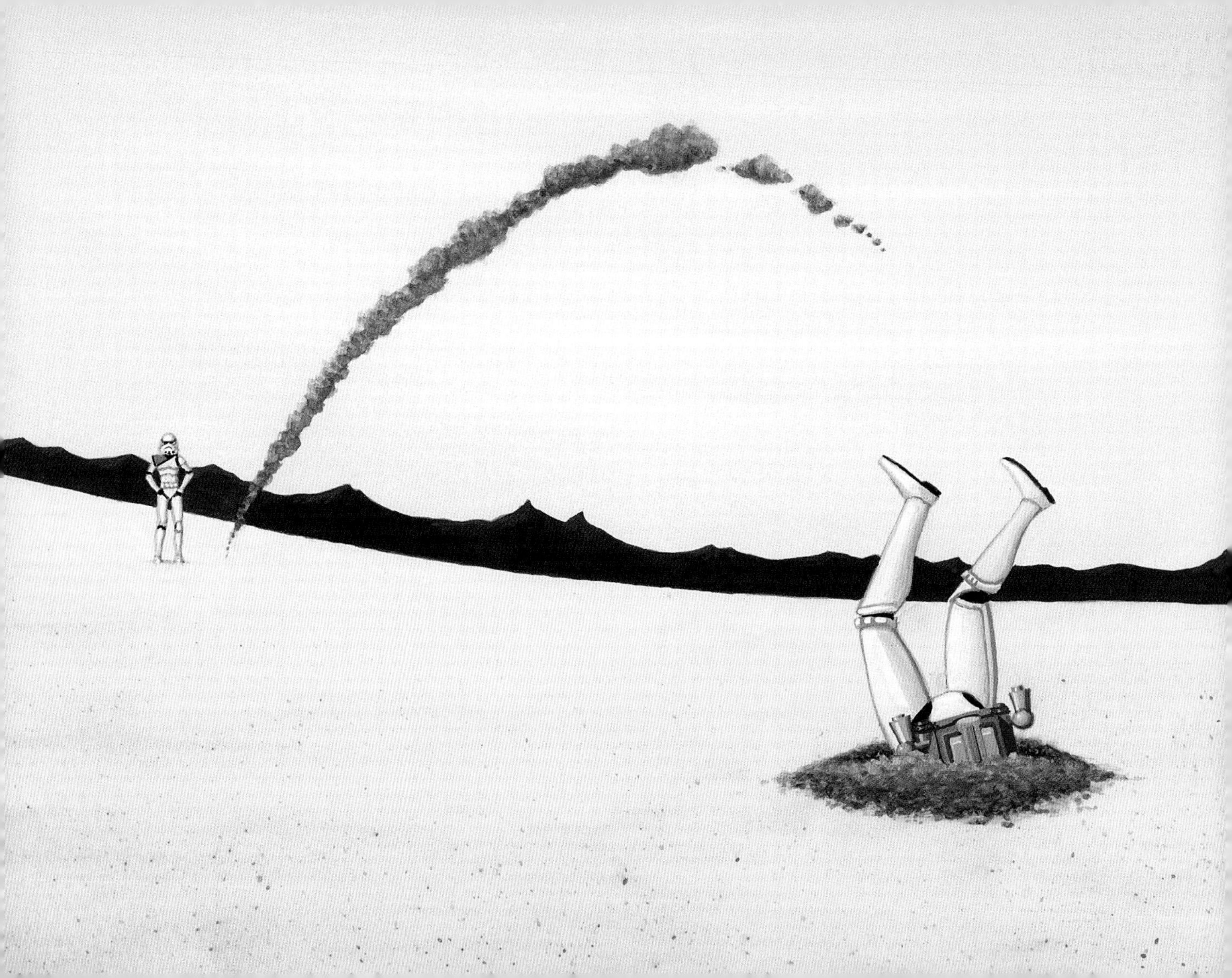

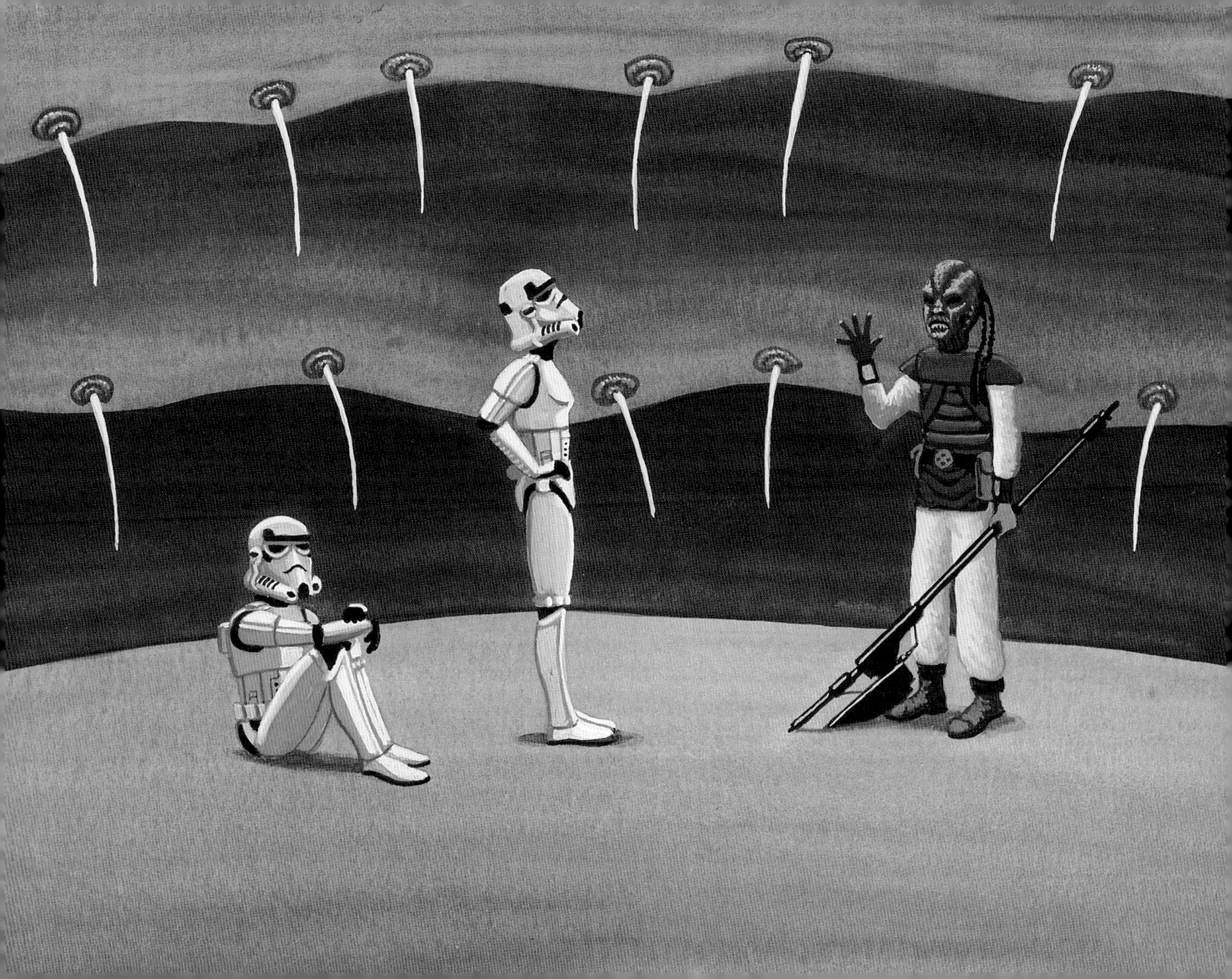

Two stormtroopers fall into the Sarlacc pit.

Two stormtroopers underestimate a princess.

70

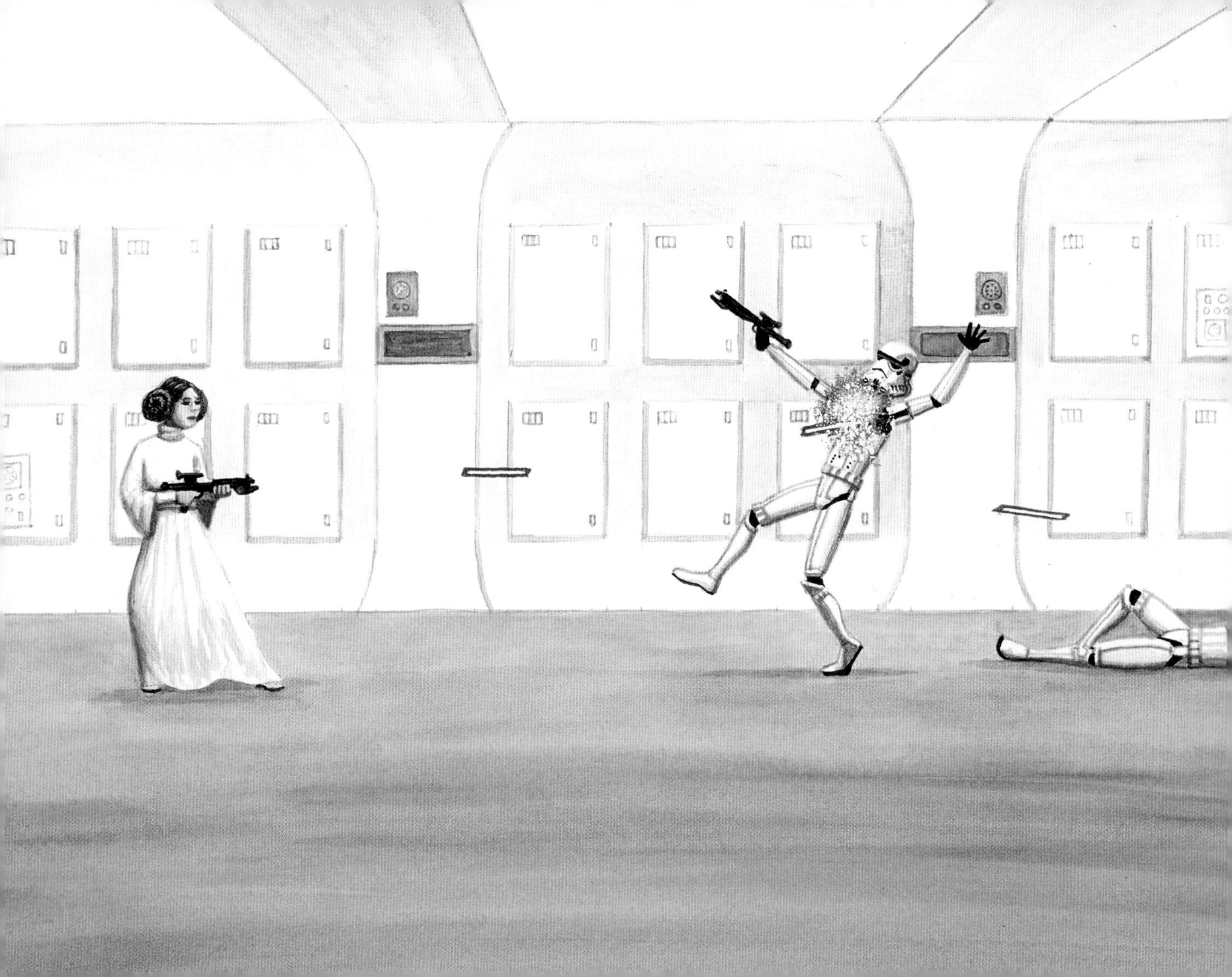

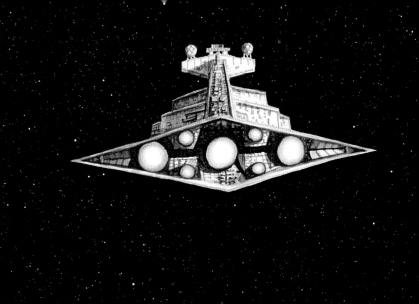

One stormtrooper asks for a promotion.

One stormtrooper falls victim to a practical joke.

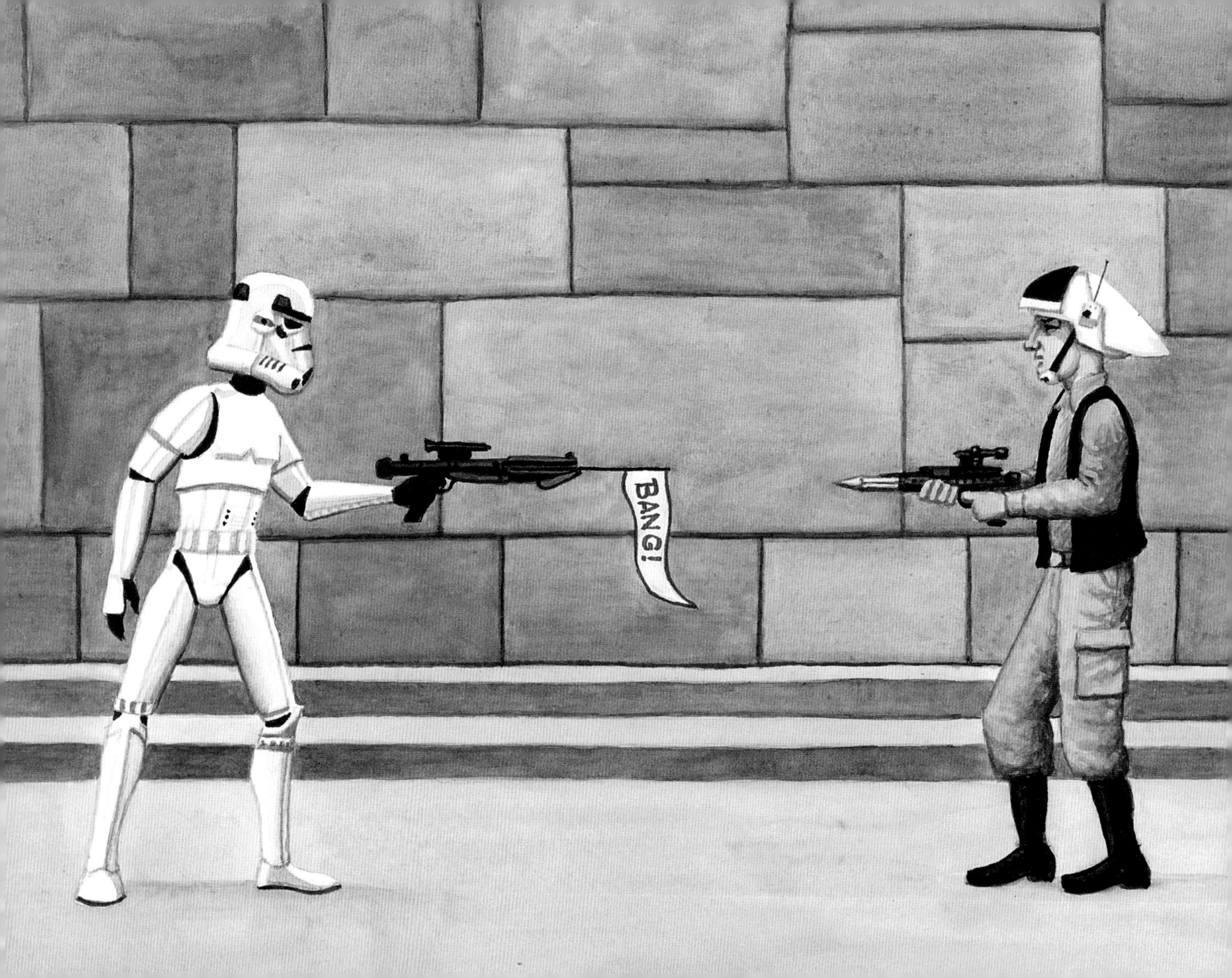
BANG!

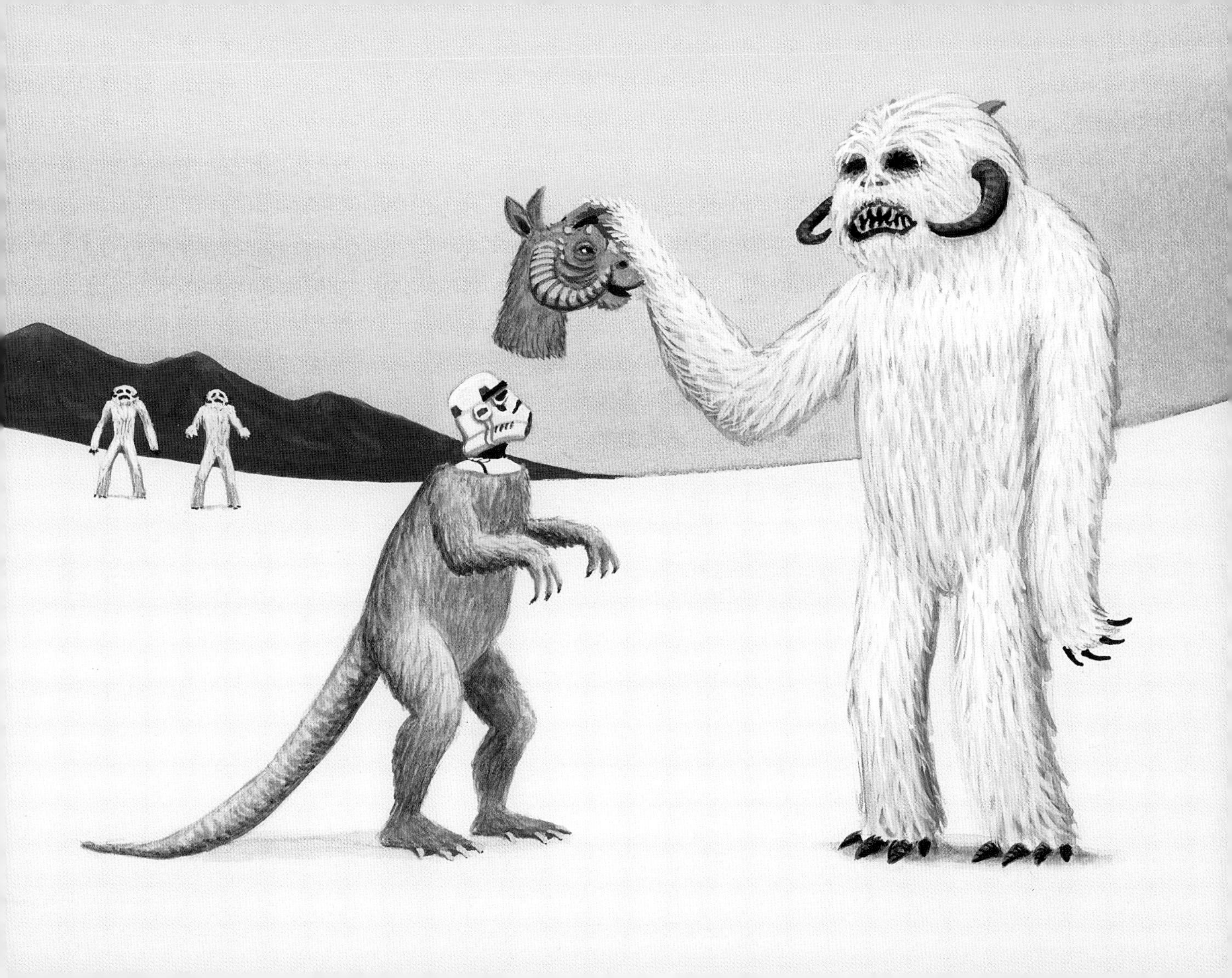

One stormtrooper tries to go undercover.

One stormtrooper doesn't look where he's going.

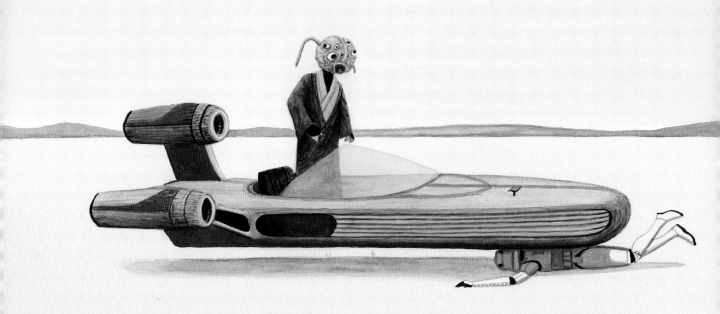

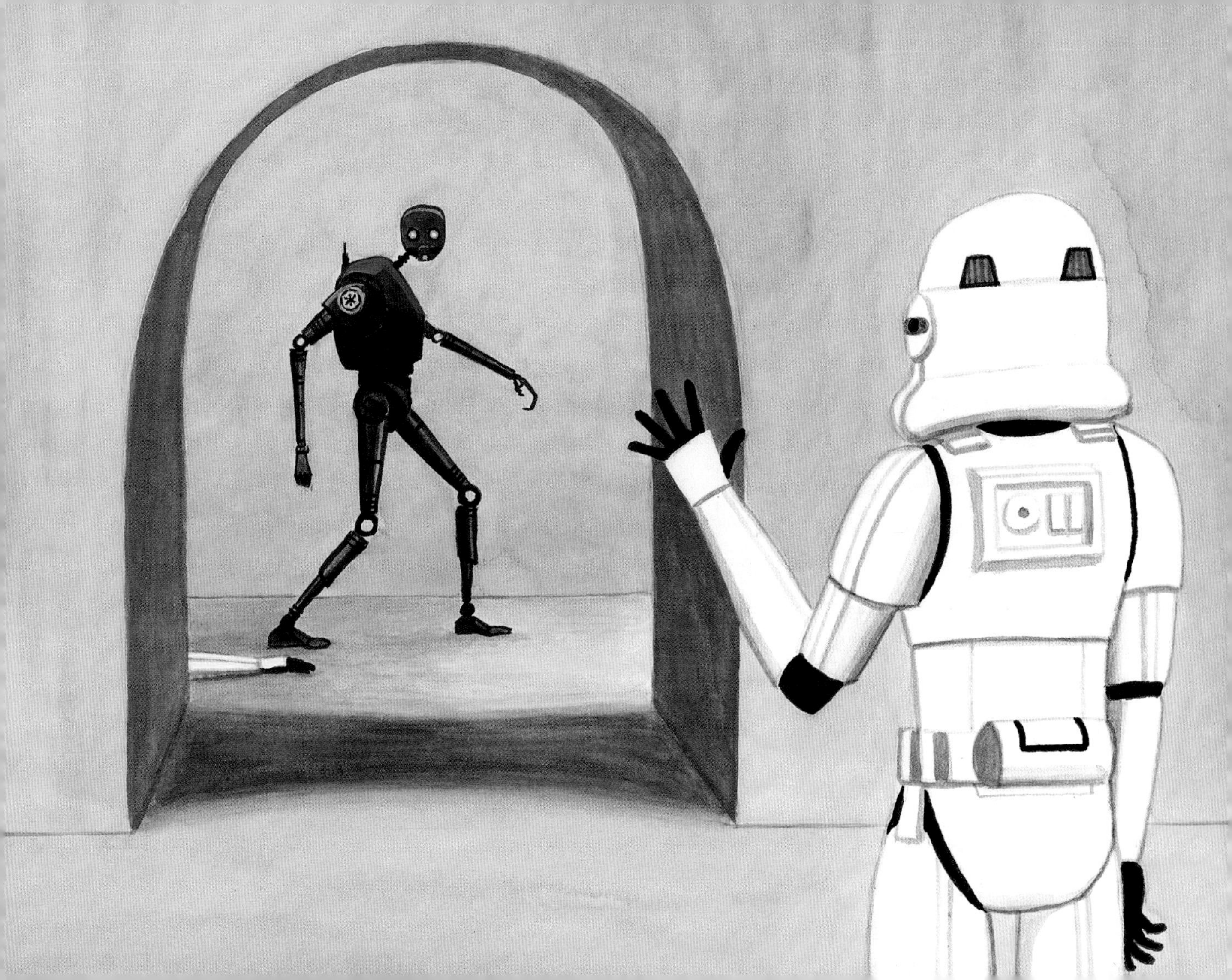

Two stormtroopers think the security droid is on their side.

Two stormtroopers go out on forest patrol.

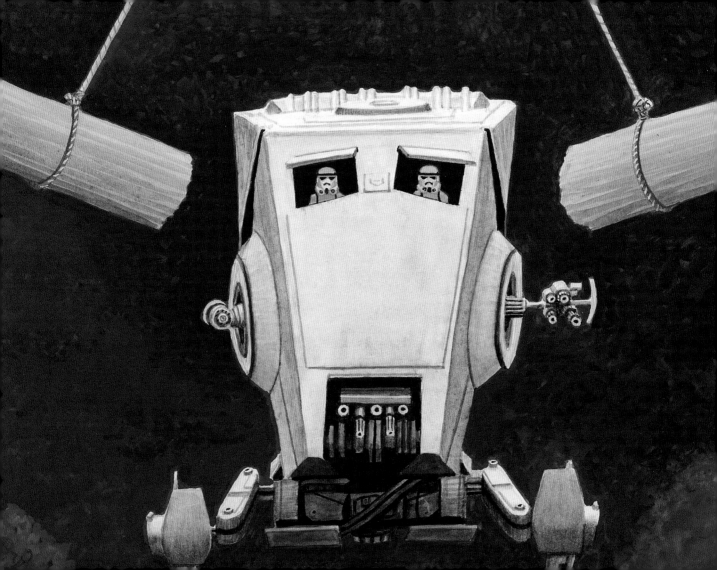

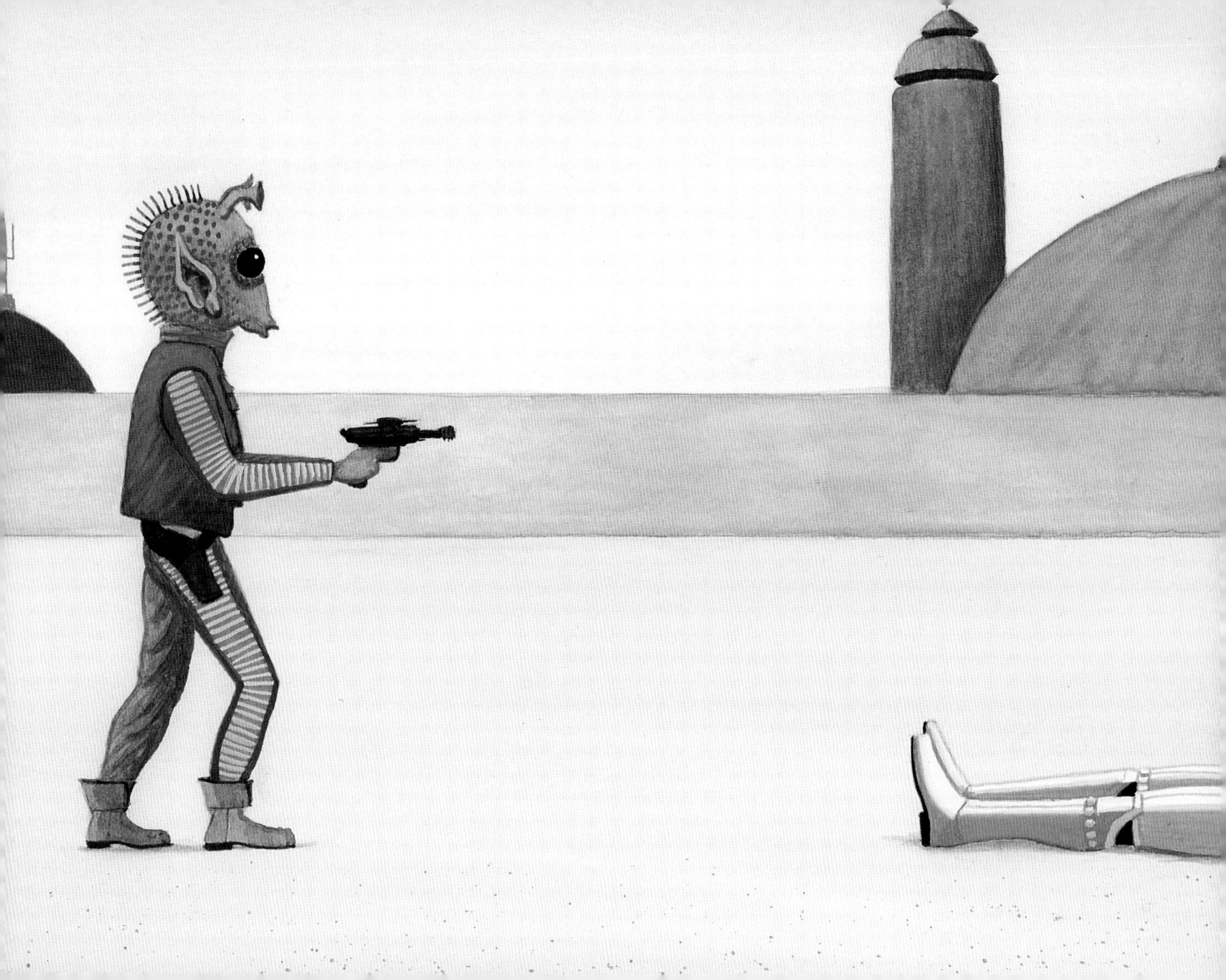

One stormtrooper fails to shoot first.

Two stormtroopers wear the wrong armor.

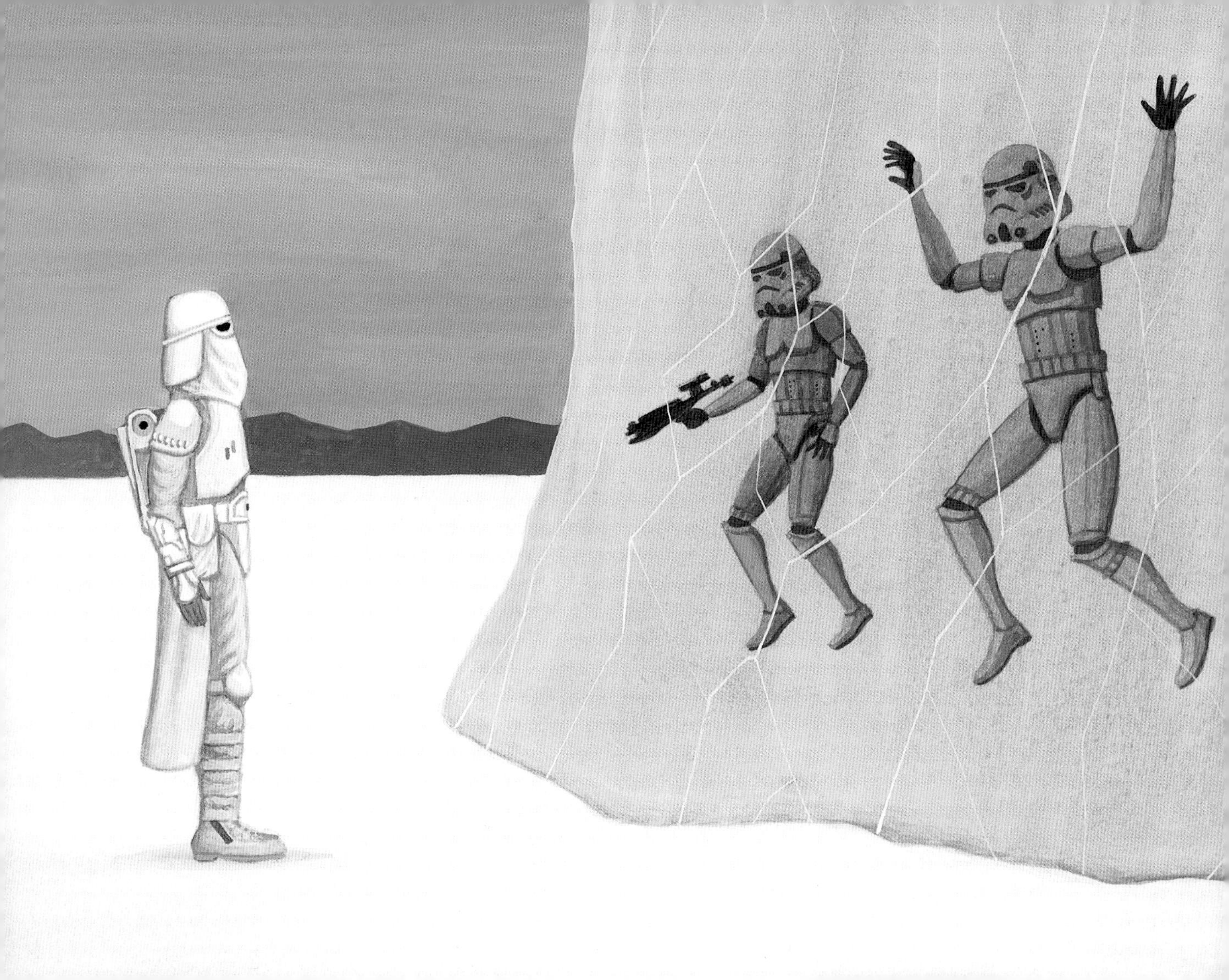

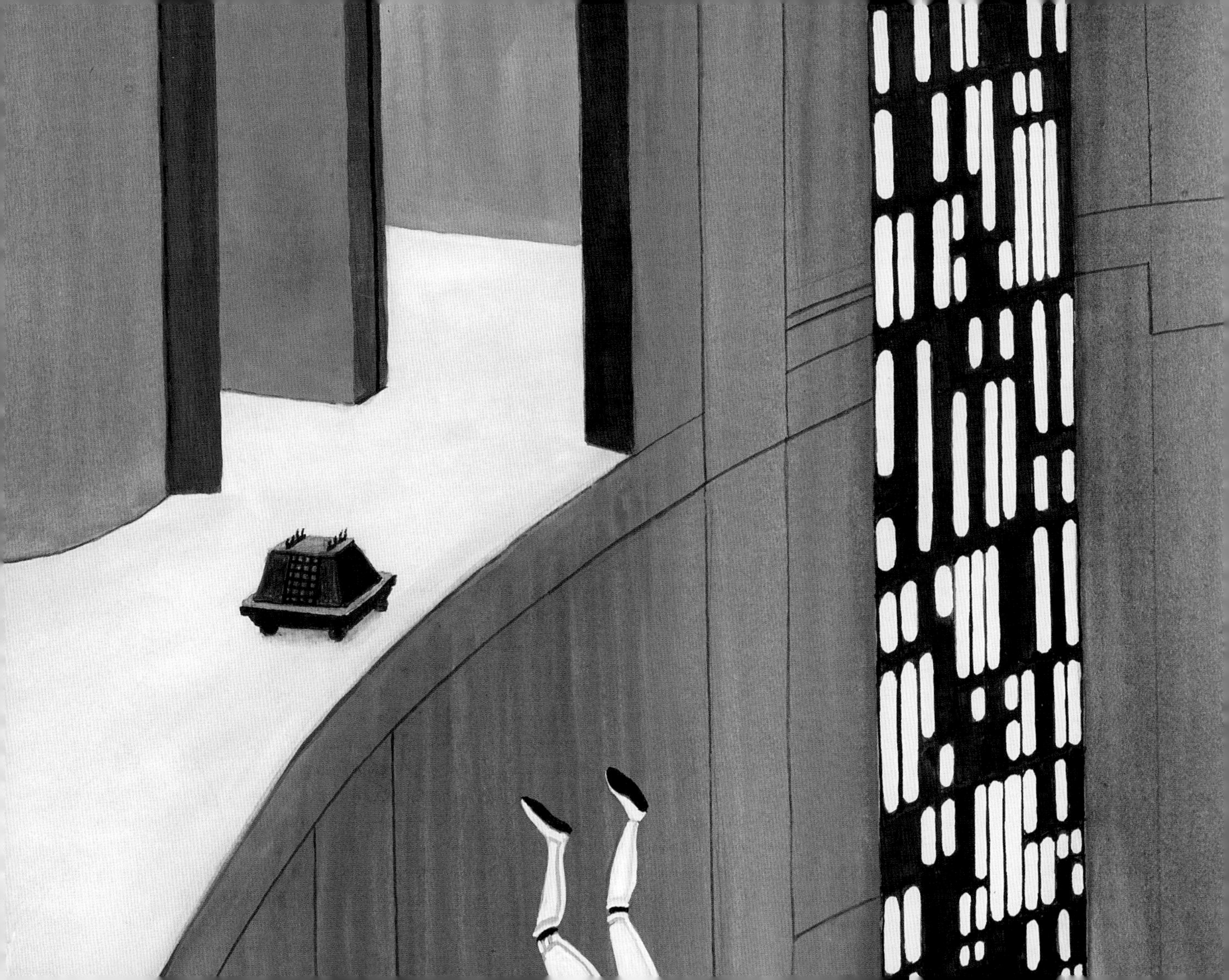

One stormtrooper is startled by a mouse droid.

One stormtrooper wishes he was a better shot.

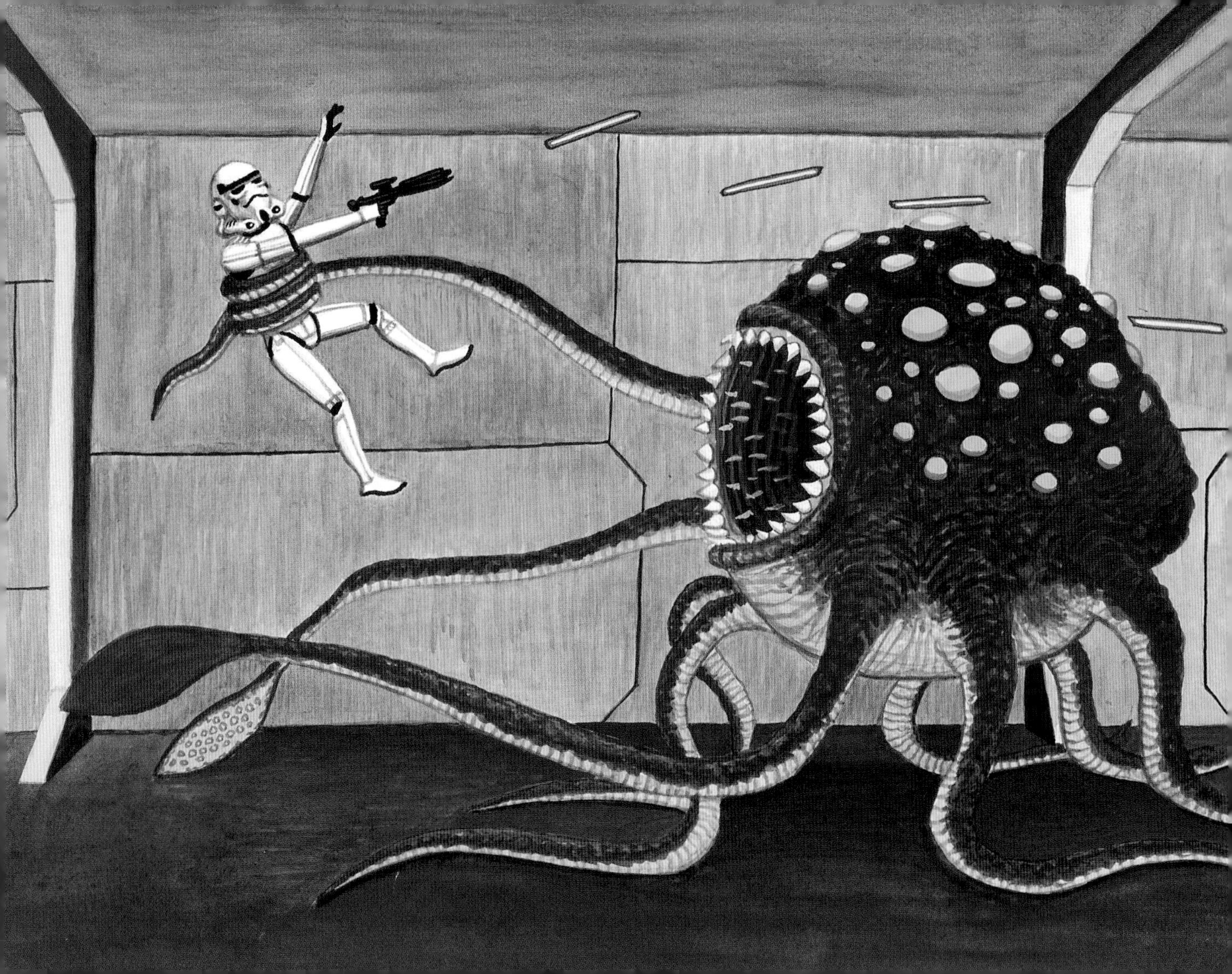

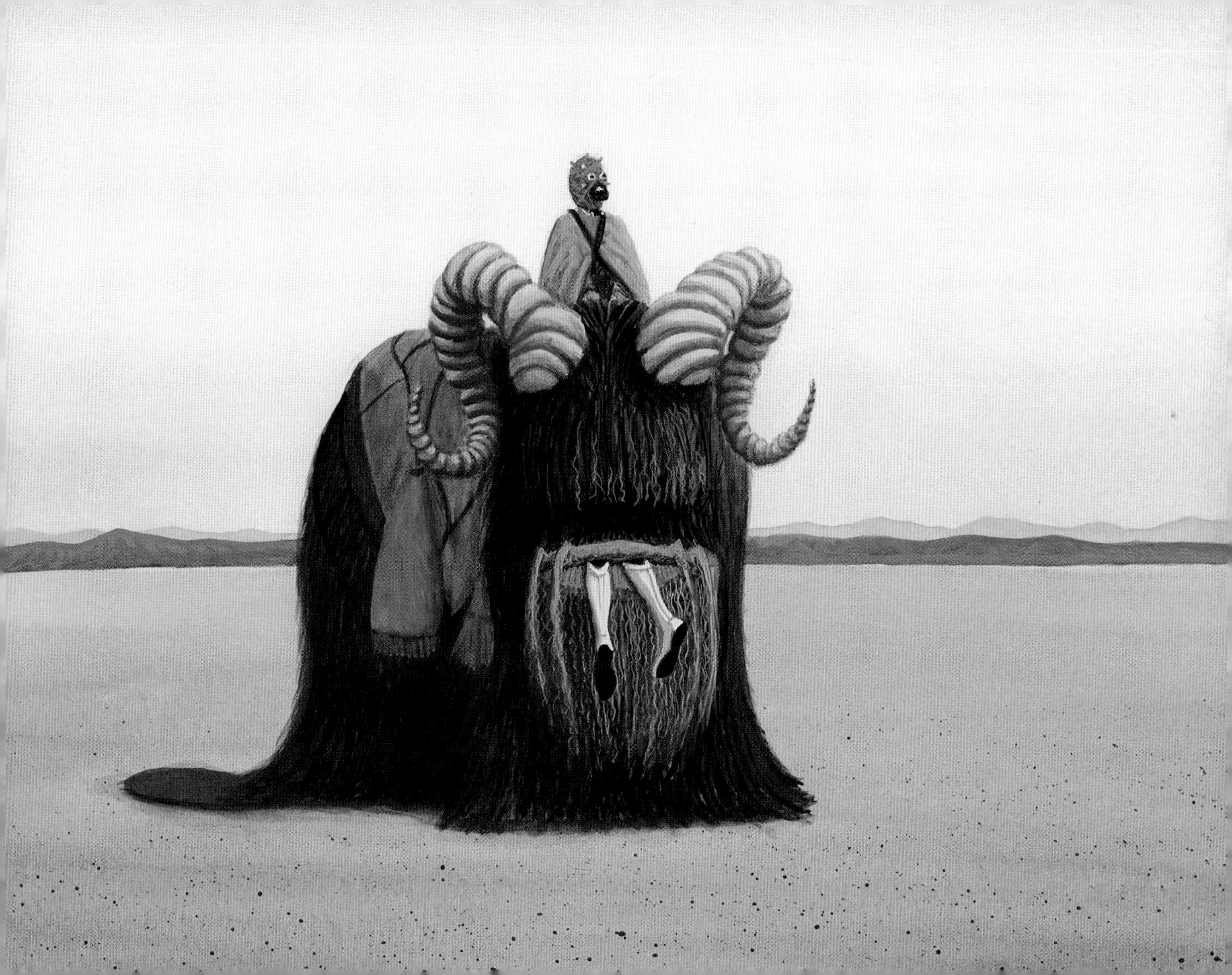

One stormtrooper becomes bantha fodder.

Three stormtroopers don't see the Jawas.

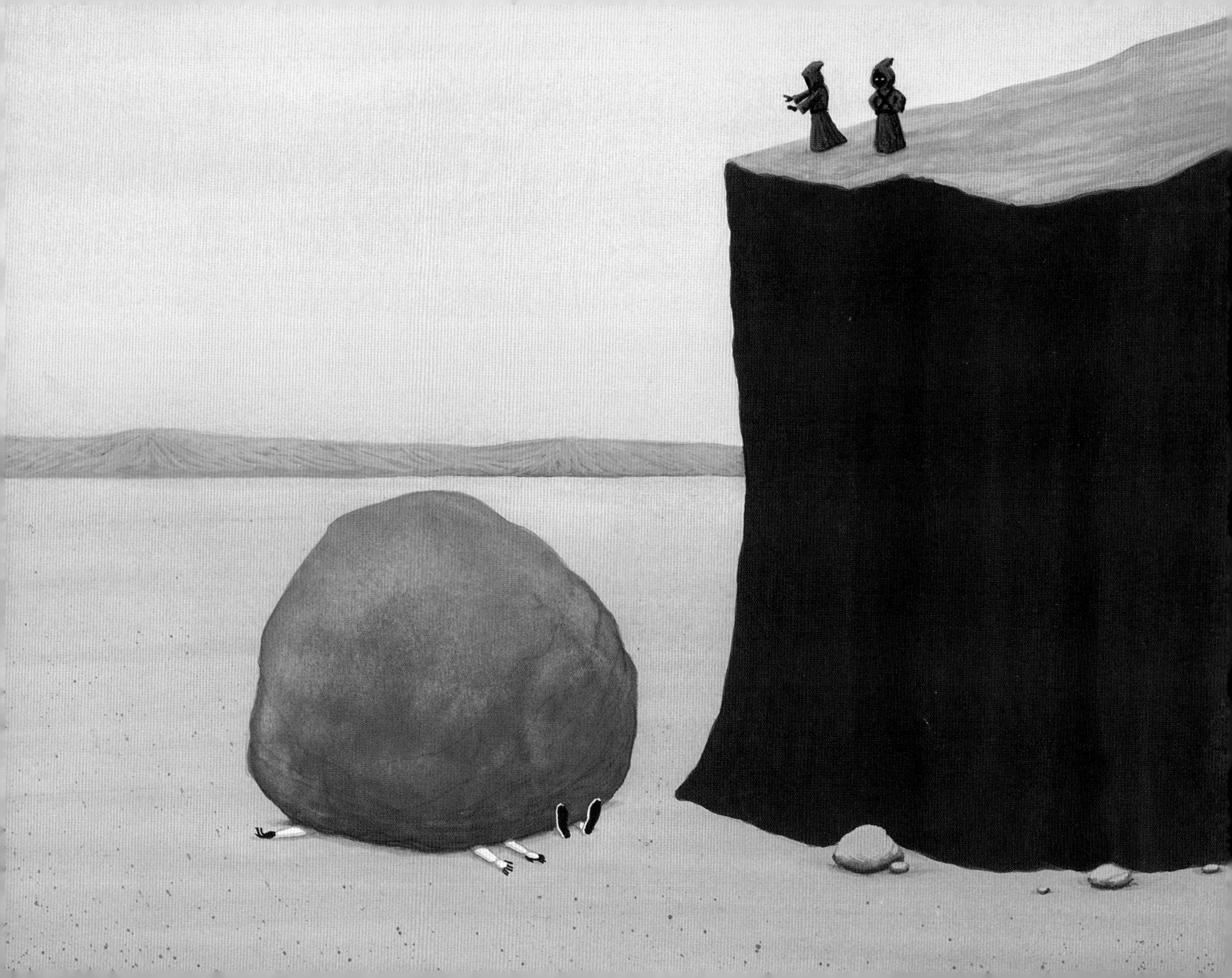

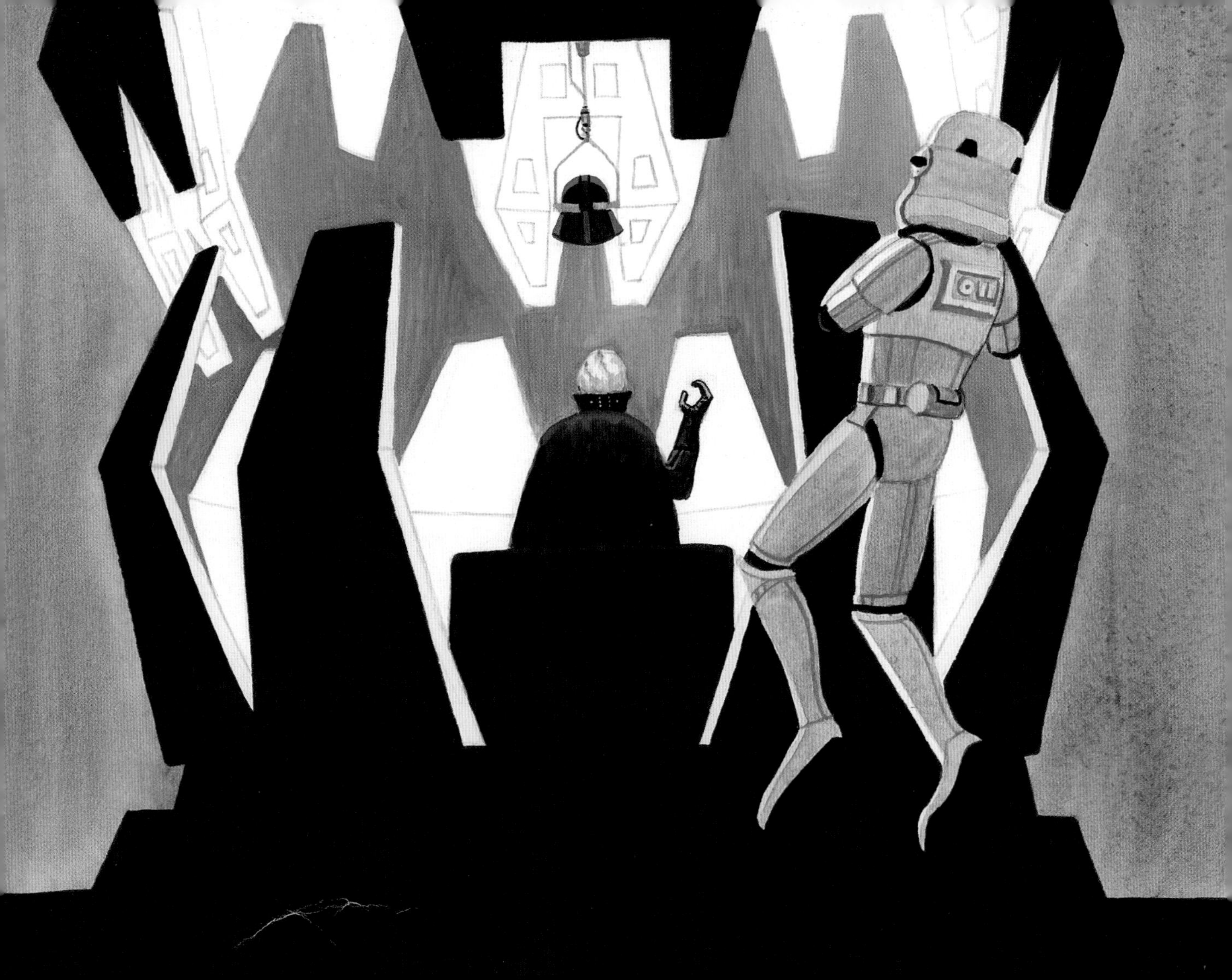

One stormtrooper disrupts Lord Vader's private time.

One stormtrooper badmouths a bounty hunter.

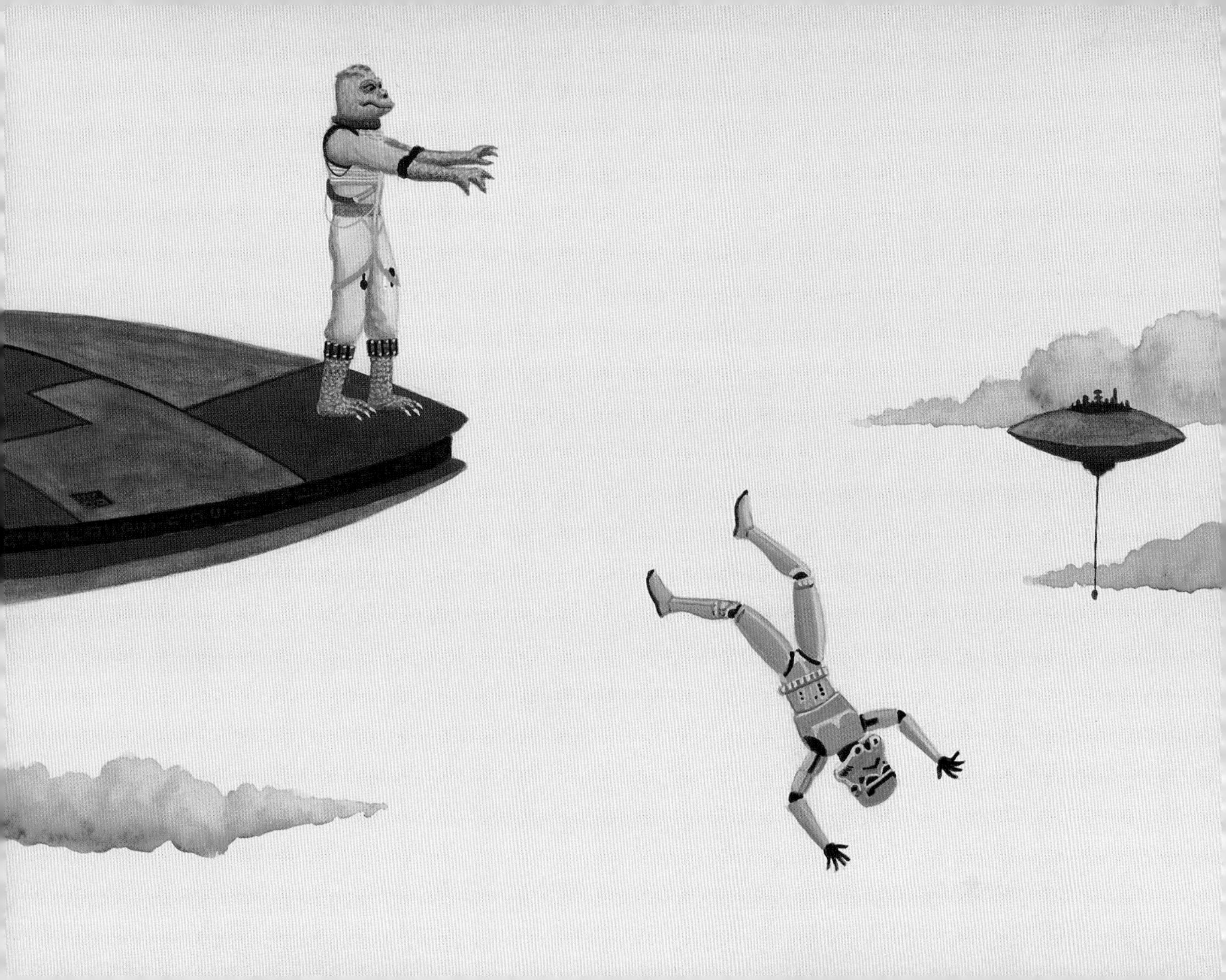

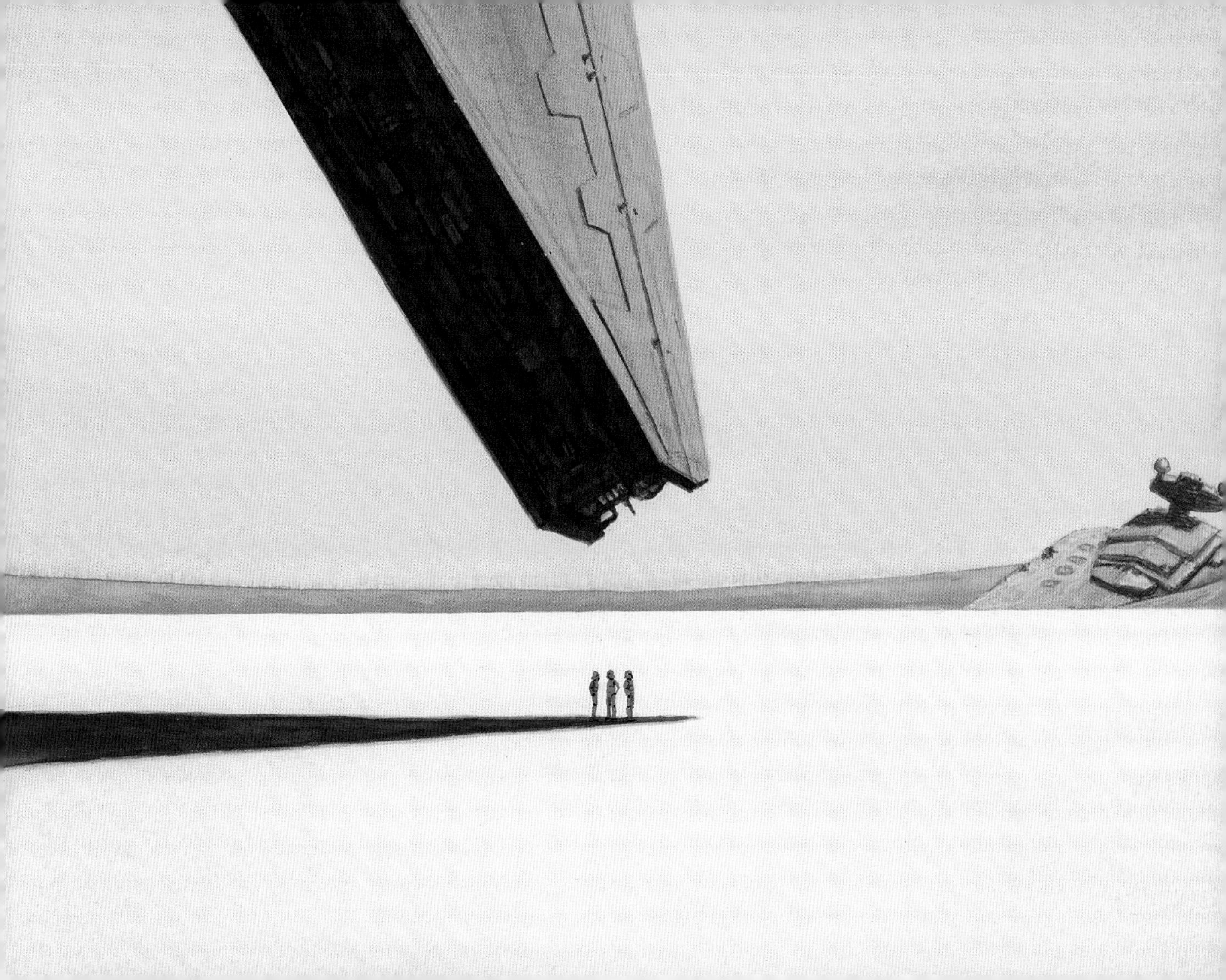

Three stormtroopers don't see the Star Destroyer.

One stormtrooper takes his lunch break in the carbon-freezing chamber.

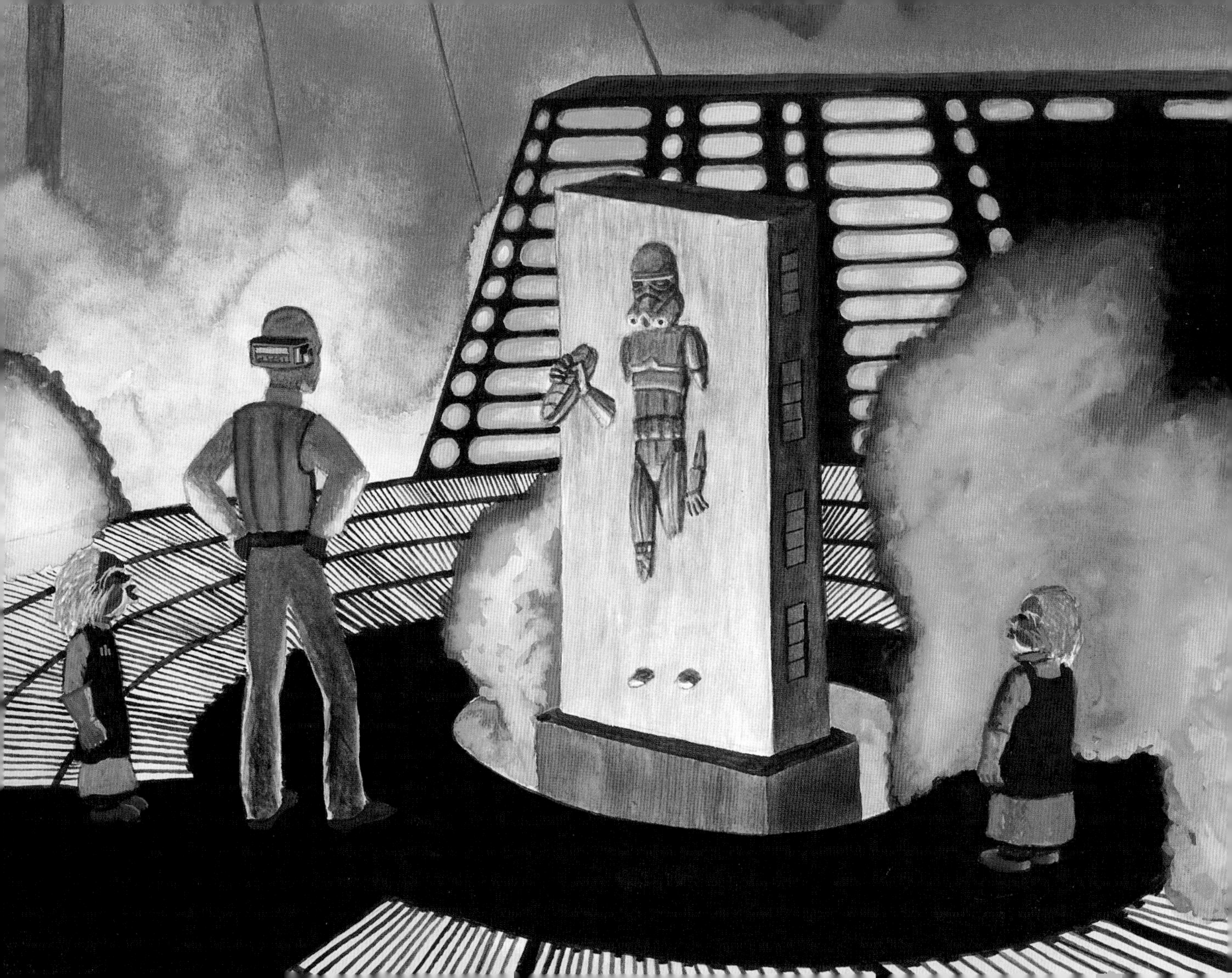

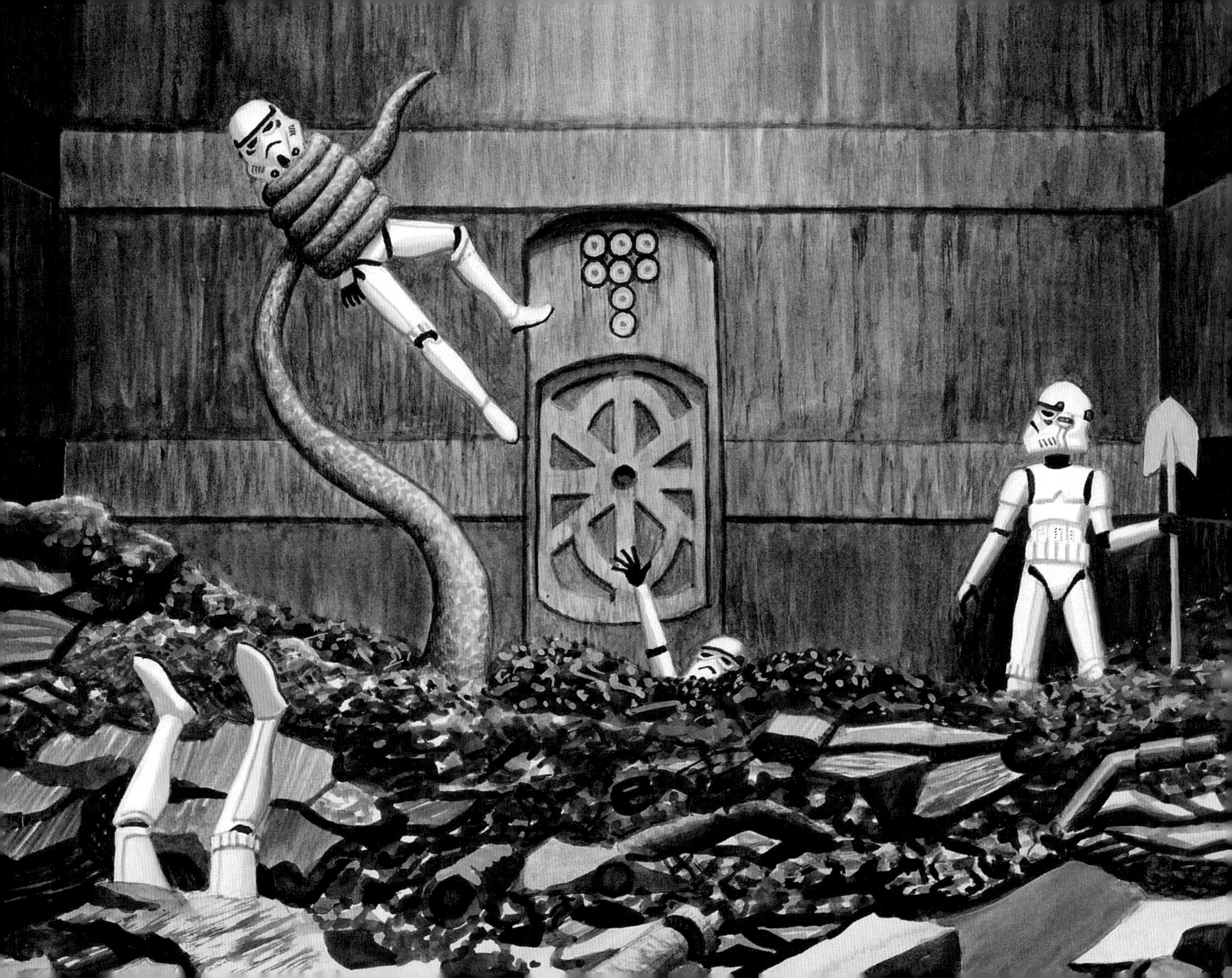

Four stormtroopers are put on garbage duty.

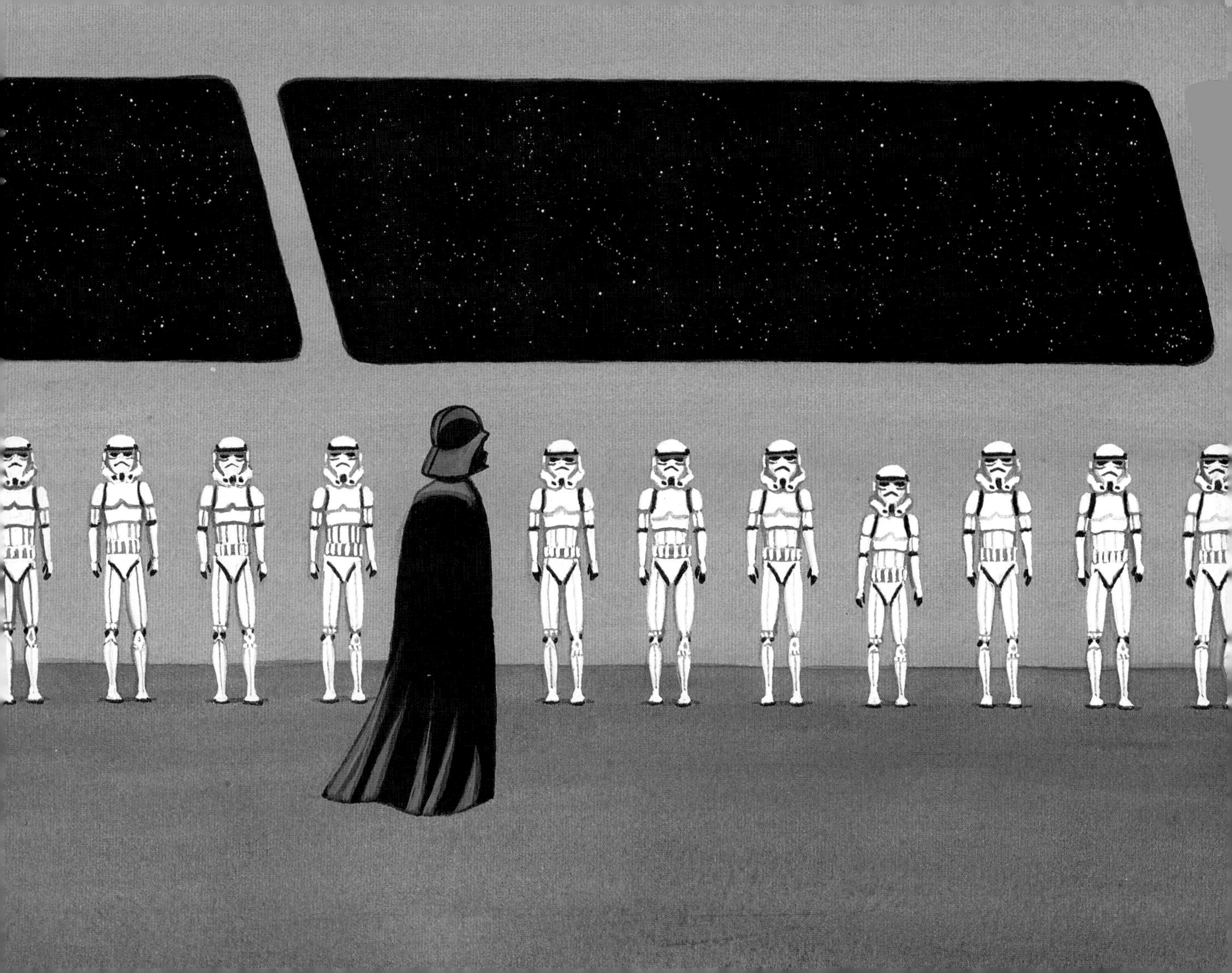

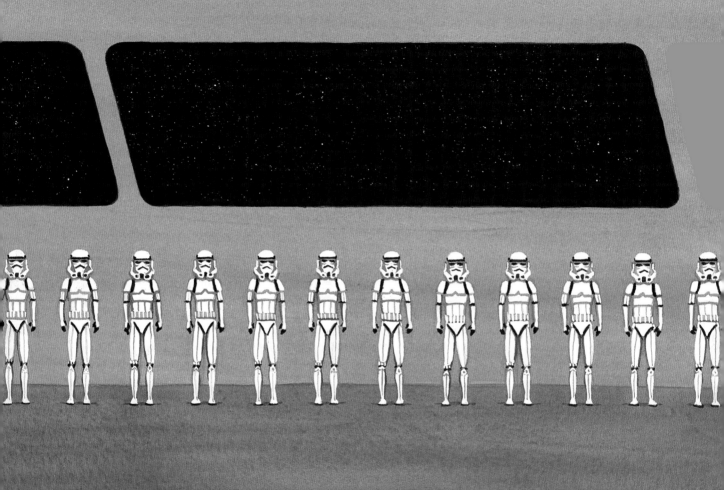

Ninety-nine stormtroopers join the Empire.

Thanks to Steve Mockus, Kathleen Kennedy, Brooke Stones, Caitlin Kennedy, the LucasFilm Story Group, Michael Morris, Beth Steiner, Lia Brown, Julia Patrick, Jeffrey Brown, Ralph McQuarrie, Andres Ainsworth, J. J. Abrams, Gareth Edwards, and, of course, George Lucas.

Library of Congress Cataloging-in-Publication Data Available.

ISBN 978-1-4521-5924-9

Manufactured in China

MIX
Paper from responsible sources
FSC™ C104723
FSC www.fsc.org

Written and illustrated by Greg Stones
Designed by Michael Morris

10 9 8 7 6 5 4 3 2 1

Chronicle Books LLC
680 Second Street
San Francisco, California 94107
www.chroniclebooks.com

www.starwars.com

STAR WARS
99 STORMTROOPERS JOIN THE EMPIRE

GREG STONES

CHRONICLE BOOKS
SAN FRANCISCO